APPLIQUÉ
THE ANN BOYCE WAY

OTHER BOOKS AVAILABLE FROM CHILTON

Robbie Fanning,
Series Editor

APPLIQUÉ
THE
ANN BOYCE
WAY

CONTEMPORARY
QUILTING

Chilton Book Company
Radnor, Pennsylvania

Copyright © 1993 by Ann Boyce
All Rights Reserved
Published in Radnor, Pennsylvania 19089, by Chilton Book Company

Illustrations by Walter Boyce
Designed by Anthony Jacobson
Manufactured in the United States of America

Library of Congress Cataloging in Publication Data

Boyce, Ann.
    Appliqué the Ann Boyce Way
        p.   cm. — (Contemporary quilting)
    Includes index.
    ISBN 0-8019-8247-2
    1. Appliqué. I. Title. II. Series.
TT779.B69   1993
746.44′5—dc20   92-56581
                                                      CIP

1 2 3 4 5 6 7 8 9 0   2 1 0 9 8 7 6 5 4 3

Contents

Acknowledgments

Alexander Henry
Bernina of America, Inc.
CM Offray & Son, Inc.
Coats and Clark (J&P Coats)
Concord House
Creative Quilting Magazine
Dritz Corp.
Elna, Inc.
Fabric Traditions
Fairfield Processing
House of White Birches
HTC–Handler Textile Corp.
New Home Sewing Machine Co.
Pfaff American Sales Corp.
Rosebar
Simplicity Pattern Co.
Singer Sewing Co.
Springmaid
Sulky of America
Talon/Tootal American
Therm-O-Web Inc.
VIP Fabrics
Vogue/Butterick Pattern Co.
VWS, Inc. (Viking)
YLI Corp.

Foreword

Ann Boyce's appliqué book emphasizes the fun of designing something uniquely personal, then takes you on a journey to create the finished product.

Her logical, forthright, step-by-step directions are easy to follow. They are interspersed with tips to simplify the process—without sacrificing style.

Ann's talents are many and her generosity in sharing ideas makes her the ideal teacher for the less than confident beginner, as well as a stimulator for the accomplished needle artist.

This new book, complete with charts for materials and tools, all identified by brand name, makes a wonderful primer. Add it to your library now, and buy an extra for the perfect gift to a creative friend.

Priscilla Miller

Why I Love to "Paint" with Fabric and Thread

In the second grade I fell in love . . . with my grandmother's sewing machine. I couldn't wait to get the treadle going at full speed. I guess that set up my love of the fast-sewing lane for life. My grandmother tried to get me to slow down; according to her, I was going to ruin her Singer. I still haven't slowed down: My sewing machines are stretched to the limit. I always look for the unorthodox path of sewing projects. I don't have a home economics degree—I guess that was too conventional for me. I have struggled between my love of art and music all my life. If I had known when I was in college where my sewing machine could take me, I guess I would not be playing Beethoven now.

I come from a background typical of the babyboom era. My love of sewing skipped from my grandmother's generation to mine. My mother does Bloomingdale's and labels—"If it's homemade, you're poor." My parents strove to give their children the best—things they didn't have growing up. But I had to be different. For as long as I remember, I sewed my own clothes with my grandmother on weekends. I didn't want to see myself turning the corner. My last acquiescence to my parents was ordering my wedding gown from Lord & Taylor. My mother would have died of embarrassment had I *made* it! Marriage freed me from that constriction. Now I sew my own clothes and don't have to explain myself.

But something is amiss: I can't sew a Simplicity pattern *as is*. I have to "junk it up." I am an individualist. I *have* to add patchwork, appliqué, decorative threads, beads, and jewels.

Come to think of it, nothing is amiss: I don't want to look ordinary. Besides, when I travel, I am an advertisement of my sewing skills. I am a curiosity on United Airlines: I wear my jackets when I travel. I learn a lot: (1) how many people sew; (2) how many people stare; (3) how many people are impressed; (4) how many people expect it of me—"Why aren't you wearing your work?" If I'm not teaching a class or attending a social function, I usually wear jeans and a blouse, with unusual jewelry for sparkle. (When I travel I collect fabrics, threads, and trims. What I once wore won't do.) I'm always seeking new ideas and designs.

Why I Love to "Paint" with Fabric and Thread

Why did I want to write this book? I hope to help take some of the mystery out of appliqué. I always look for what's missing. "How do you sew that?" "Will my machine do *that*?" I don't want to see another "ducks and bunnies" pattern book: I want to explain how your machine will *make* those ducks and bunnies. I want you to do something creative on your sewing machine, to individualize your clothing and quilts.

Not long ago I was invited to attend an award ceremony in New York City for the American Print Council. Now that I have a life of downward mobility, I knew I couldn't afford to buy a dress to wear to a lah-dee-dah New York event. If I did, I would look like someone from *Hee-Haw*. I am a designer, a sewer, a creative person. I sewed up a jacket with Concord fabrics and glitz. A man complimented my jacket. Better yet, I won the award and went onstage to accept my trophy. Oddly, it was a rarity to see a home-sewn outfit at an event in the sewing industry! I was proud to say, "I made it myself."

INSPIRATION FOR APPLIQUÉ

Introduction

Using the sewing machine to paint pictures with thread and fabric is an "Open Sesame" for a creative sewer. Fabrics, threads, and trims will spin together into a web of colorful designs and textures.

Creative sewing time is at a premium. Today's busy home sewer can accomplish creative projects in a fraction of the time it took our ancestors; and even the newest technology in sewing machines is constantly changing. We can draw pictures on the screen of our home computers and the Pfaff 1475CD will sew them. New Home's Memory Craft 8000 can sew elaborate embroidery stitches with only a touch of both a cassette and a button. New Home also has a scanner to scan patterns and reproduce them with thread. Viking's 1A will satin stitch in four separate directions. Singer's Quantum XL will sew decorative stitches 25 mm (1") wide and Pfaff's 1475CD will sew stitches 40 mm (1½") wide. All of the new machines will sew literally hundreds and hundreds of decorative stitches. Bernina has over 50 different sewing machine feet, easing virtually every application. The choices and possibilities are endless.

We can direct these possibilities into creative sewing projects by using various fabrics, threads, and notions. The same project can look totally different with two separate sets of supplies; one can be understated and subtle, while the other can be glitzy and outrageous.

This book is a primer on sewing machine techniques and applicable accessories and products. I have given many distinctive projects and patterns only as a suggestion for application of the design. The same techniques can be used with other designs. My intent is to take the fear, trepidation, and hesitation out of trying new sewing machine techniques. There are pattern sources everywhere: try magazines, books, greeting cards, wrapping paper, calendars, and fabrics. The shapes can be traced, copied, enlarged, reduced, and drawn.

Be forewarned: There are copyrights on most designs. For appliqué shapes you need to have the outer shape as a guide. While it would be difficult to duplicate the design on a greeting card exactly, it should only serve as inspiration for your own interpretation.

ANN'S TIP. Never use trademarks as a design (e.g., Disney characters); they are licensed, and copying them may precipitate a lawsuit brought on by some wicked witch.

Don't be afraid to mix and match a wide variety of fabrics: try velvet, silk, corduroy, cotton, blends, metallics, and synthetic leathers and suedes.

Refer to my book, *Putting on the Glitz,* and *Claire Schaeffer's Fabric Sewing Guide,* also published by Chilton, for extensive information on handling different fabrics.

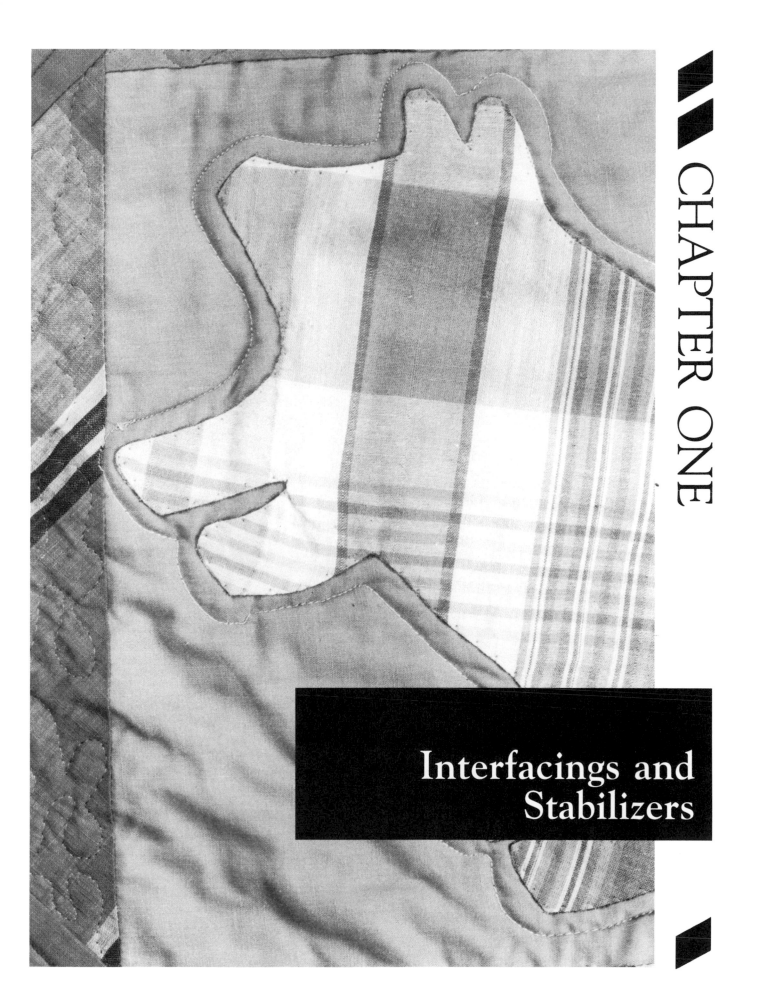

CHAPTER ONE

Interfacings and Stabilizers

Some projects in this book use products that fuse and stabilize fabrics. There was once only a loose fusible web, with many drawbacks: it is very hard to draw on; it shifts easily, so is difficult to position; it gunks up your iron's soleplate; and it comes in only one weight. In order to fuse this product, you must use a Teflon sheet on one side to prevent the web from melting onto the wrong surface.

Still, it has some redeeming qualities: I use it to repair a pulled-out hem; to hold down a loose facing; to repair a tear in fabric; or to fuse synthetic or real suede or leather seam allowances open.

There is now a product far superior to the loose fusible webbing. This webbing is bonded on one side to a piece of smooth paper. You can easily draw and mark the paper; fuse the web onto the wrong side of fabric; cut out the shape; peel off the paper; and fuse the shape in place. This product is sold under several brand names, including Pellon Wonder-Under, Dritz Magic Fuse, HTC Trans-Web, Staple Transfer Fusing, and Aleene's Hot Stitch Fusible Web.

There is another product similar to this paper-backed fusible webbing, manufactured by Thermo-Web and called Heat 'n' Bond. Instead of fusible webbing layered with paper, this product is a thin sheet of solid glue. It is also available in rolls of different widths for appliquéing ribbons and strips of fabrics. *Be careful* to purchase Heat 'n' Bond *Sewable* or *Lite*. The heavier product, Regular Heat 'n' Bond, is for craft and nonsewable projects. It will gunk up the sewing machine needle and cause thread to fray and/or break.

There are several brands of stabilizers you can use for the techniques throughout this book: Pellon Stitch 'n' Tear, HTC Armo Tear-Away, Sulky Totally Stable.

For fusible knits, try Dritz Quick Knit/Knit Fuse, Stacey Easy Knit, Staple French Fuse, Pellon Knit-shape, or HTC Fusi-Knit.

For 100% cotton, use Dritz Classic Woven, Stacey Shape-Flex, Staple Shapewell, or HTC Form-Flex.

I often use fabric glue stick or spray adhesive for *temporary* fusing. Alternative products for stabilizing include Reynolds freezer paper, typing paper, tissue paper, Palmer/Pletsch Perfect Sew, and all brands of wash out water-soluble stabilizer (solvy).

Other supplies you'll need on hand for machine appliqué are sharp-pointed embroidery scissors, Gingher appliqué scissors, tweezers, iron cleaner and fusible thread (see Chapter 3). In the back of this book you'll find some sources for these and other sewing products.

Interfacing Chart

J & R	STACY	STAPLE	PELLON	HTC	DRITZ
Fuse 'N Use		Jiffy Fuse		Stitch Witchery	Stitch Witchery
Quick Knit	Easy Knit	French Fuse	Knitshape	Fusi-Knit	Knit-Fuse
Stretch 'N Shape	Easy Shaper Lightweight	Jiffy Flex	EasyShaper	Fusi-Form	Shape-Up Lightweight
Classic Woven	Shape-Flex All Purpose	Shapewell		Form-Flex All Purpose	Shape-Maker All Purpose
Soft 'N Silky		Shape Up		So Sheer	
Tailor Fuse		Fusible Suitmaker		Armo Weft	Suitmaker
Magic Fuse		Transfer Fusing	Wonder-Under	Trans-Web	
Shirtbond		Fusible Shirt Maker	ShirTailor	Armo Shirt-Shaper	Shirt Maker
Craf-T-Back			Craftbond	Crafters' Choice	
Create A Shade			Decor Bond	Fuse-A-Shade	Shade Maker
Bridal Shape		Woven Durable Press		Veri-Shape Durable Press	
Woven Form		50/50 Durable Press		Sta-Form Durable Press	Sew-In Durapress
Craf-T-Fleece	Thermolam Plus	Poly-Fluff		Armo Fleece Plus	Big Fleece
Fusible Craf-T-Fleece				Fusible Fleece	Press-On Fleece

CHAPTER TWO

Quilting with Cotton
and Cotton-Blend
Battings

All the appliqué projects in this book use cotton or cotton-blend battings exclusively. The batting is a medium to enhance machine arts rather than just a quilt filling. It is used as a stabilizer; as the inside of three-dimensional appliqué; and for warmth in clothing and quilts. The use of cotton battings opens up a whole new territory for elaborate sewing machine artistry.

The easiest and best-looking results for machine decorative and appliqué stitches and for elaborate quilting derive from using natural fibers. The cotton and cotton-blend battings "stick" to the wrong side of the fabrics. They do not shift or bunch up when you sew through them.

There are several cotton and cotton-blend battings on the market: Fairfield Cotton Classic—80% cotton/20% polyester; Mountain Mist Blue Ribbon—100% cotton; Warm 'n' Natural—100% cotton; Hobbs' Heirloom—80% cotton/20% polyester; Morning Glory—100% needlepunched cotton. See chart for selection guide.

One of the cotton-blend battings, Fairfield Processing's Cotton Classic, can be split in half. Start at the corner and gently pull apart to separate the batting into two halves.

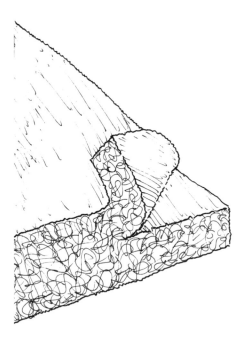

ANN'S TIP. Splitting Cotton Classic gives you twice the batting for the money.

Place the soft side of the split batting against the wrong side of the fabric to be quilted (the stiffer, bonded side will be on the outside). Using half a layer of Cotton Classic will make your garment softer and more drapable. A quilt with a half-layer of batting will have a feel similar to that of an antique quilt. This lighter weight is particularly desirable for both garments and quilts in warmer climates.

Battings should always be cut at least 1″ larger than the quilt project. If you use a backing, you should cut it at least 1″ larger than the batting.

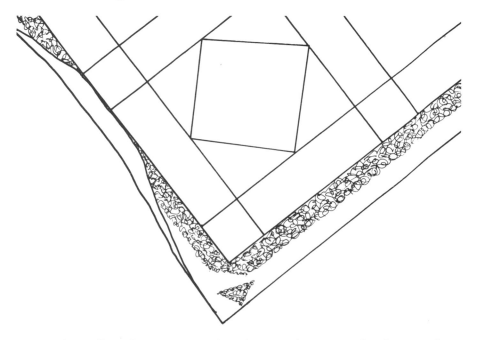

After all quilting is completed, trim the excess backing and batting flush with the top, unless you are binding a quilt with my method (see Chapter 11).

All my garments that have batting are free-lined (putting in the lining as the last step). I like the look, and they wear more comfortably. The appliqué and quilting are done with only the cotton batting beneath the surface layer. Don't worry that the batting will be chewed up in the feed dogs: Cotton batting will not do this.

After your garment pieces are quilted, construct the garment as you would any conventionally lined garment—the lining will be free from the outer garment.

13

ANN'S TIP. Instead of the conventional clothing linings, I use non-slinky linings, generally cotton or poly-cotton blends.

Cotton and cotton-blend battings have a variety of washing instructions. It is mandatory that you read the package for appropriate care. Various combinations of washed/unwashed components can yield attractive results. The shrinking of one of the components can give an antique look.

Several possibilities for combinations:

TOP	washed	unwashed	unwashed
BATTING	unwashed	unwashed	washed
BACK	washed	washed	unwashed

ANN'S TIP. Experiment with small 12″ quilted square samples to determine the look you like.

Two other *expensive* battings can be used for this work: silk batting is thinner, and wool batting is thicker.

If you use thicker polyester battings for quilting, the results will be puffier. Polyester battings make elaborate machine quilting harder to do. They should be used in winter outerwear, such as ski jackets. Thicker battings require much less quilting: You can leave unquilted areas up to 6″ between quilting lines. Thicker synthetic battings will compress, but they are hard to roll up and maneuver inside the arm of the machine while you are quilting. Hawaiian quilts are traditionally batted with polyester to avoid mildew in a tropical climate.

Batting Chart

BRAND NAME	FIBER CONTENT	SIZES AVAILABLE	QUALITIES
Poly-fil Traditional [1]	100% polyester needlepunched	36 x 45", 45 x 60", 72 x 90", 90 x 108", 120 x 120"	Handles like a blanket, shows fine quilting
Poly-fil Ultra-Loft [1]	100% polyester needlepunched	45 x 60", 72 x 90", 81 x 96", 90 x 108"	Extra thick for warmth. Hard to hand quilt
Poly-fil Low-Loft [1]	100% polyester	45 x 60", 81 x 96", 90 x 108", 120 x 120"	Bonded, tiny stitches possible
Poly-fil Extra-Loft [1]	100% polyester	All sizes except 36 x 45"	Used for comforters, bonded
Cloud Lite [2]	100% polyester	All sizes except 36 x 45" and by the yard	Resin-bonded, low loft
Cloud Loft [2]	100% polyester	45 x 60", 81 x 96", 90 x 108", 120 x 120"	Hi-loft, resin bonded
Poly-Down [2]	100% slick hollow-core polyester	Same as immediately above	Easy quilting, less bearding
Poly-Down DK [2]	Same as Poly-down	90 x 108"	Gray color for dark fabrics
Thermore [2]	100% polyester	27 x 45", 54 x 45", 45" roll	Thin, no bearding, for clothing
Heirloom [2]	100% polyester needlepunched	45" wide by the yard	Good for unusual sizes
Resin-bonded polyester [2]	100% polyester	48" to 96" wide by the yard	Available in thick and thin lofts
Mountain Mist [3]	100% polyester	All sizes including 36 x 45"	Soft, good for first project
Quilt-Light [3]	100% polyester	45 x 60", 81 x 96", 90 x 108"	Small stitches, thin batting
Fatt Batt [3]	100% polyester	72 x 90", 81 x 96", 45 x 60", 90 x 108"	Extra thick, Glazene finish
Mountain Mist Cotton [3]	100% cotton	81 x 96", 81 x 108"	Bleached, Glazene finish
Blue Ribbon Cotton [3]	100% cotton	90 x 108"	Can quilt 2" apart, lightweight
Cotton Classic [1]	80% cotton, 20% polyester	81 x 96"	Blended to resist bearding
Warm & Natural [4]	100% cotton	90 x 90"	Unbleached, specks visible
Heartfelt [5]	100% wool	60 x 90", 80 x 90", 90 x 90", 90 x 108"	Needlepunched, soft, 1/2" thick
Taos Mountain Designer Light [6]	100% wool	36 x 84", 72 x 94", 80 x 90", 90 x 94", 94 x 108"	Needlepunched, thin, drapes
Taos Mountain Traditional [6]	100% wool	Same as immediately above	Can be tied in 8 – 10" intervals

1. Fairfield Processing Corporation   2. Hobbs Bonded Fibers   3. Stearns Technical Textiles Co. (Mountain Mist)
4. Warm Products, Inc.   5. Heartfelt   6. Taos Mountain Wool Works

CHAPTER THREE

Threads for Appliqué

Metallic Thread

When I made my first Fairfield Fashion Show garment in 1984, the only metallic thread colors I could find were gold and silver. Now the range of colors is extremely wide, and the threads come in textures from fine to coarse, from several manufacturers:

Dritz	Madeira
DMC	Mez-Alcazar
Gütermann	Sulky
J&P Coats	Talon
Janome	Tire
Kanagawa	YLI
Kreinik	

When I wrote *Putting on the Glitz,* my knowledge of using these metallic threads pertaining to needle size was limited to standard needle sizes and types. Since then I have learned that the Schmetz regular topstitching needle (80/12, 90/14, or 100/16) has a larger scarf. This needle will virtually eliminate metallic thread breakage and burring.

The blue coating you find on some needles is a Teflon coating. This type of needle is helpful in gliding through the fabric if a topstiching needle is not readily available.

I used to use only standard sewing thread colors in the bobbin to match the upper metallic thread color. If your bobbin-thread color shows to the front of the fabric, you can use a thin metallic thread in the bobbin. Lower the upper tension on all machines to facilitate metallic thread sewing. Don't be afraid to lower the tension further if necessary (#5 to #2 in some extreme cases). This may prevent the bobbin thread from showing on the top.

ANN'S TIP. If you have a Bernina, you can use regular thread in the bobbin without show-through if you thread through the finger on the bobbin case.

Sometimes metallic threads will spin off the spool as you are sewing. All machines sew these threads differently. You need to keep trying on samples until you find a method for your machine.

ANN'S TIP. Feed metallic thread around the bobbin winding spool on an Elna 9000 for smoother feeding.

ANN'S TIP. If your machine has both a horizontal and an optional upright spool holder, such as on a New Home or a Viking, use the upright holder for metallic threads.

Before threading the sewing machine needle, smooth out any twists or kinks in the loose metallic thread. If the thread breaks, repeat this smoothing out process before rethreading the needle. Sometimes painting stripes on the actual metallic thread with a lubricant such as Sewer's Aid will help this thread to sew well.

ANN'S TIP. Thread metallic threads through the metallic thread guide on the right rear of the handle of a Bernina.

The ends of the plastic spools used by both Sulky and Kreinik for their metallic threads will pop up. When you have finished sewing, you can wind the thread around that end of the spool and snap it shut, locking the thread. Read the symbols on the spool ends of Madeira metallics to determine whether your sewing machine can handle it.

Always sew relatively slowly with metallic threads. I warn my students that if they sew metallic threads "pedal to the metal," it is at their own risk. Sewing too fast may cause metallic threads to break.

All metallic threads can be used on the upper looper of a serger (overlock machine) for decorative effect. Metallic Wooly Nylon thread is now available for decorative serging. Some thinner metallic threads, such as *Glamour* (Madeira), can be used in both the upper and lower looper. Metallic ribbon floss can also be used in the loopers.

Transparent Monofilament Nylon Thread

There are two colors of monofilament thread, clear and smoke. The darker smoke color should be used on darker fabrics; the clear on lighter fabrics.

Many companies manufacture or distribute monofilament thread:

Clotilde	Talon
J&P Coats	Treadleart
Nancy's Notions	YLI
Speedstitch	

This thread is usually used in the needle; cotton or polycotton thread is usually used in the bobbin. If you cannot adjust the bobbin tension to keep the bobbin thread from showing on top, a metal bobbin can be filled to capacity with monofilament thread. If your machine uses only plastic bobbins, fill them only half full of monofilament, as the plastic bobbin can explode if it is completely filled.

If your machine has problems stitching or feeding the monofilament thread, experiment with the following solutions:

- The best weight for monofilament thread is fine. If this breaks in your machine, switch to the next heavier weight.
- Thread the machine normally and lower the upper tension slightly.
- If you have a newer Bernina, thread the monofilament through the metallic thread guide on the machine's handle.
- Use the alternate vertical spindle found on some machines, such as New Home and Viking.
- Put a drinking straw in the center of a larger cardboard core on the spool.
- Cover the monofilament thread spool with thin plastic mesh, available in sewing stores or by mail. J&P Coats' brand serger spools are sold with a fabric covering you can use with monofilament thread.
- Place thread in a clear glass jar either next to or behind the machine. Cover thread in jar with plastic mesh.
- Purchase a separate metal thread stand. Try it either to the side of or behind the machine.
- Use masking tape to attach a large-eye hand sewing needle to the top of the machine with the eye toward the back of the machine. Feed thread through this eye.

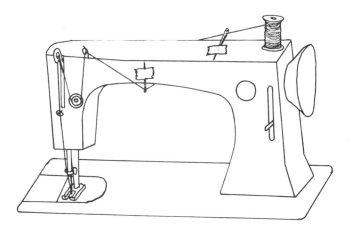

- Feed thread in an unorthodox path: between the spindle and the take-up hook; around a bobbin winder; around another parallel spindle or through the bobbin winding guide, where applicable.

- Hang thread from the ceiling. (Special hooks are available.)

- Put thread on the floor behind or to the right of the machine. It may have to feed through a separate thread stand in addition to this.

1. Be extremely careful of discarded monofilament thread clippings. They can be dangerous and even fatal to children and animals if ingested.

2. Cut ends are scratchy to the skin. One solution is to cut extra length ends and "hide" the ends using a hand sewing needle.

3. Do not use a direct iron on monofilament. Use lower heat and press either with a press cloth or on the wrong side—if you used regular thread in the bobbin.

Rayon Threads

Rayon threads are available in a wide range of colors, both solid and variegated, and are available from a number of manufacturers:

Janome	Natash
J&P Coats	Sulky
Madeira	Talon
Mez-Alcazar	

These threads are easy to sew on the machine. They are intended for decorative machine stitching. Do not, however, sew seams together with rayon thread: It is not strong enough for construction sewing.

Rayon thread can be used both on top of the machine and in the bobbin. It is more economical to use utility cotton or polyester in the bobbin. Sometimes the balance is not correct on a machine and the bobbin thread will show to the front. To correct this, lower the upper tension slightly.

ANN'S TIP. On a newer New Home Memory Craft, set the upper dial from "auto" to "light weight."

On occasion the rayon thread will spin off the spool or catch on the spool. In that event, flip the spool upside down on a vertical spool, or backwards on a horizontal spool. Use the metallic thread guide to help even feeding of the thread.

If you are appliquéing a heavier fabric, such as Ultrasuede or denim, with rayon thread, use a larger needle (14/90 or 16/100) to pierce the fabric. Rayon thread may break with a smaller needle size.

Silk Thread

Silk is the most expensive thread. It can be used both in construction and for decoration. The 25% natural elasticity of the silk filament makes this thread perfect for all types of fabrics. It is thinner than conventional threads and will not leave holes in fabric—a quality particularly nice for basting.

There are several sources for silk thread:

Belding Corticelli   Singer
Gütermann   Tire
Janome   Zwicky (only topstitching)
Simplicity

Use a 9/70 sewing machine needle with fine silk thread; a 90/14 or 100/16 needle with silk topstitching thread.

It is best to use a fine thinner thread in the bobbin, such as Mettler's (Metrosene) 100% Egyptian cotton embroidery thread. It is manufactured in a wide range of 120 colors, and will closely match the color of the silk thread.

Acrylic Thread

New Home/Janome developed an acrylic thread to use on their Memory Craft 8000 machine. It is stronger than rayon thread and has the high sheen of rayon. The embroidery feature on the Memory Craft 8000 is self-sewing: That is, the machine sews by itself with no pedal. It sews the embroidery motifs at varying speeds, so a thread that could sew without breaking at any speed was necessary. This thread is available in 24 colors and has a companion thin white polyester thread specifically designed for the bobbin. This bobbin thread does not show on the front of the embroidery.

Although this acrylic thread was developed especially for New Home, it can be sewn on all machines.

Machine-Quilting Threads

There are only a couple of specific machine-quilting threads. Machine quilting is possible with most types of threads: monofilament, cotton, poly-cotton, metallic, and silk. Special machine-quilting thread is a heavier weight, which showcases the quilting stitches. One manufacturer is Mettler/Metrosene. They make a 100% cotton thread. There is less snagging, knotting, and breaking through all the layers of a quilt or quilted garment with this 100% cotton thread. The other manufacturer of machine-quilting thread, Tootal/Talon, makes a cotton-covered polyester thread. Both brands sew easily with a 14/90 needle, both threads can be used with regular utility-sewing thread in the bobbin, and both have a luster that is subtle in the finished quilting project.

ANN'S TIP. Do not use wax-covered hand-quilting thread in the machine.

Fusible Thread

There are a couple of 100% nylon fusible threads: Threadfuse and J&P Coats' Stitch 'n' Fuse. These are heavy white threads that will melt when pressed with an iron. Use these threads only in the bobbin; use regular thread in the needle.

This fusible thread is used to hold down edges of fabric or seams. You can sew around an appliqué shape with fusible thread on the wrong side; when you press it in place, the melted thread will hold the appliqué for later conventional appliqué sewing. This eliminates the need for fusible webbing, which makes fabric stiffer.

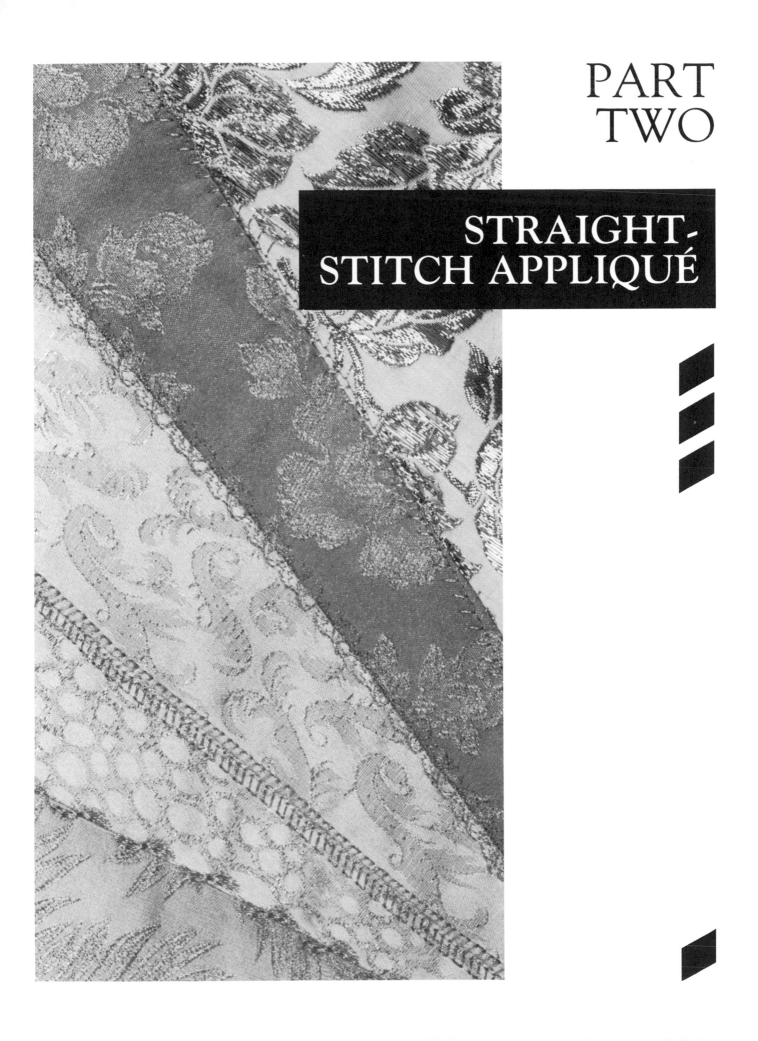

PART TWO

STRAIGHT-STITCH APPLIQUÉ

CHAPTER FOUR

Straight-Stitch Appliqué on Printed Fabric

Straight-Stitch Appliqué

I teach a class called "Sewing Machine Savvy," a one-day introduction to three kinds of appliqué and machine quilting. Without fail, someone shows up with an old black Singer Featherweight machine. It generally sews only straight stitch, although once a student brought a mechanism that attaches to the presser foot and wriggles the stitches sideways to *loosely* resemble machine appliqué. For my straight-stitch sewing machine victims only, we have to appliqué with a straight stitch—when you get a lemon, make lemonade! This is a primitive alternative to other methods of machine appliqué, but it provides a special look nonetheless. Several years ago, I asked Marinda Stewart to make me an appliquéd pig jacket out of Concord's feed sack fabric. The pig logo on the back of the jacket is appliquéd with straight stitch.

Here is my method:

1. Trace your appliqué template onto the fabric with a silver Berol pencil.

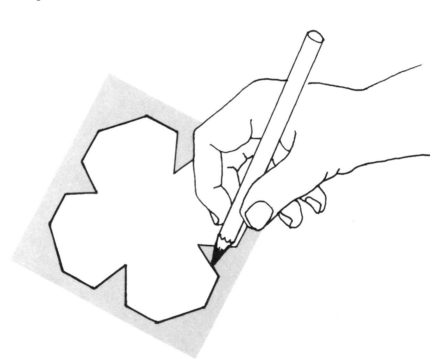

2. Cut out your appliqué design allowing an extra ¼″ of fabric outside the drawn outline.

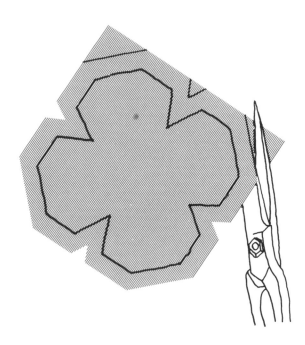

3. Straight stitch around the design *on the drawn line*. Clip the curves and inside points, and trim the outside points, to the stitched line.

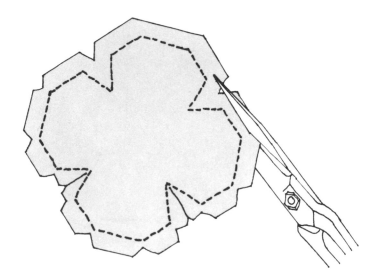

4. Turn under and press all edges, barely rolling the stitched line to the underside. It's helpful to use spray adhesive or glue stick to hold the edges under.

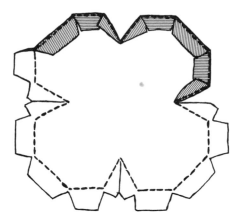

5. Set machine to a regular straight-stitch length (10 to 12 stitches to the inch, or 2.5). Topstitch around the appliqué very close to the outside edge. (Use monofilament thread in the needle if you don't want the stitching to be visible.)

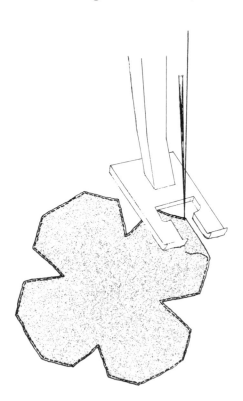

ANN'S TIP. Use an edge-stitch foot for even stitching.

CHAPTER FIVE

Award-Winning Piped
Appliqué Jacket

The fabrics in this jacket are left over from Concord fabric I used to make up a home decorating room setting for a trade show. I needed a jacket to wear on a business trip to New York, so I used the scraps and sewed this up to wear. Concord later entered the jacket in an American Printed Fabrics Council Tommy Award competition and it won a trophy in the "apparel" category.

Choosing a Pattern

A loose-fitting, Oriental style pattern works best for this type of jacket. Look for a pattern that has a simple banded collar. Consider a pattern with no darts. This jacket was constructed onto the reverse side of the cotton lining fabric and later serged together to finish the inside seams.

Getting Started

All the appliqué will be done on the wrong side of the lining fabric, which will serve as the base and will also show on the inside of the finished garment. I like to use 100% cotton for lining. Cut out the lining fabric about 1″ larger all around than the pattern sections.

MATERIALS

Jacket pattern

Various fabrics for outer jacket

Cotton lining fabric and thread to match

Cording

Piping fabric and thread to match

Fabric for appliqué and thread to match

Zipper foot

Pinking shears

Rotary cutter, plexiglass ruler and mat (optional)

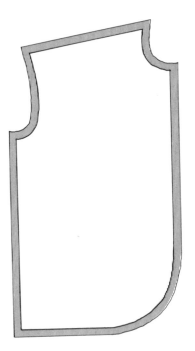

Sew all pieces onto the lining with thread that matches the lining. Color-coordinate the lining fabric with the outside fabrics.

Making Piping

The piping used in this project is about ⅜″ to ½″ wide. You will need to purchase between 6 and 7 yards of cording. I used tissue lamé.

ANN'S TIP. For this garment, soft, 100% cotton cording is preferable to the stiffer poly-cotton cording.

---

1. Cut the piping fabric on a 45° angle into bias strips. The width of the strips is 1″ wider than the measurement of the cording. For example, for ½″ piping, cut strips 1½″ wide. If you are using tissue lamé for your piping, there is no right or wrong side to the fabric. Many rotary cutter mats have 45° angles printed on them, making these ideal tools for this step.

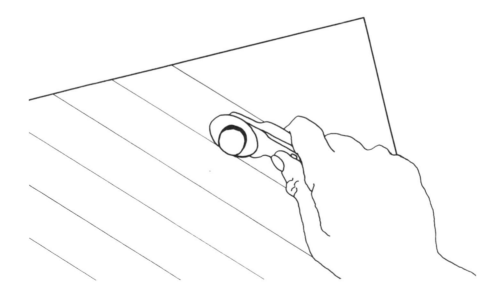

2. Sew strips together end-to-end, right sides together. When you pin two diagonal pieces together forming a "V", the outside tips should extend ¼″ on either side. These are "dog ears."

ANN'S TIP. An assembly-line chain method to sew the strips together is illustrated below. Stitch together the first two strips and continue a thread chain after the seam is sewn. Without clipping this chain, stitch together the other end of one of those strips with a third strip. In this way make one continuous strip. When finished, clip the thread chains between the seams.

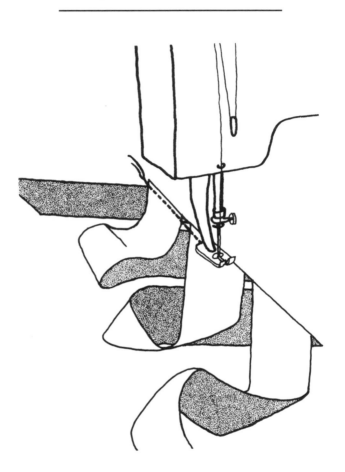

3. Press seams open.

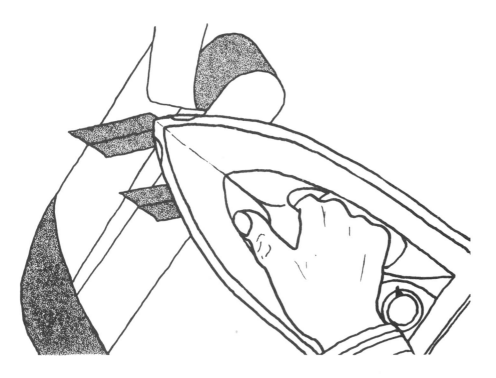

4. Trim off "dog ears."

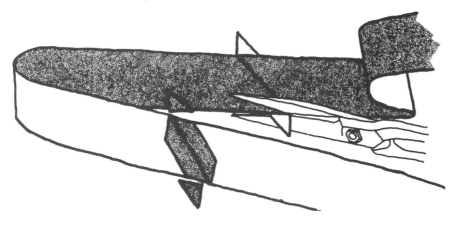

5. Attach a zipper foot to your machine and set the machine to a medium stitch length (10 to the inch, or 3.0). Thread the needle and the bobbin in a color to match the piping fabric.

ANN'S TIP. If you are using metallic tissue lamé, thread the machine in yellow for gold lamé or grey for silver. You do not need metallic thread for this application.

---

6. Fold the prepared bias strip around the cording, right side out, and stitch close to the cording, keeping the raw edges even.

37

Preparation of Motifs

1. If the fabric has distinctive shapes, such as circles or octagons, cut out these shapes at least 1″ larger than the outside edge of the design.

2. Use this cutout as a pattern to cut a second piece of coordinated fabric to use as a lining.

3. Right sides together, pin the two matching pieces together. Thread the machine in a matching color and with the wrong side of the motif facing up, straight stitch around the entire motif.

4. Cut off excess fabric to ⅛″ from stitching line, or use pinking shears to automatically trim and notch the edges.

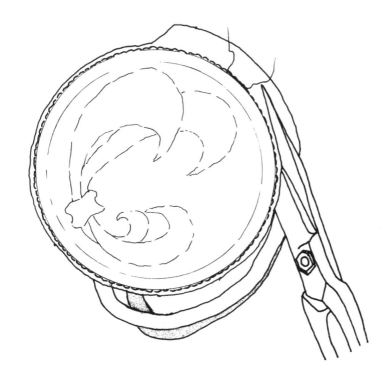

5. Slit the center back of the lining, taking care not to cut through the motif, and turn the motif through to the right side. Work the seams smooth with fingers and press.

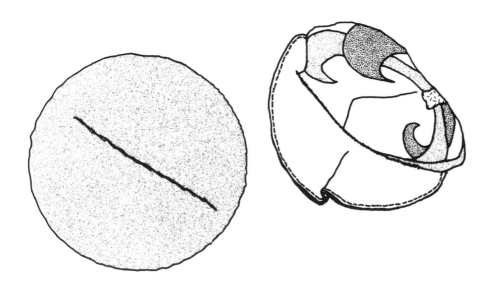

ANN'S TIP. Press with the motif face down on the ironing board so you can be sure that no lining shows on the edge of the motif.

---

6. For straight-of-grain striped-motif bands of fabric on the sleeves, simply cut extra seam allowance on the bands. Press under the seam allowance to form a finished edge.

Inserting Piping on Bands

1. Start at the top of the sleeve. Cut a strip of fabric about 8″ wide and lay the first band of fabric over the lining sleeve top, *wrong* sides together. Stitch ⅛″ from the edge of the lining to join the band and sleeve.

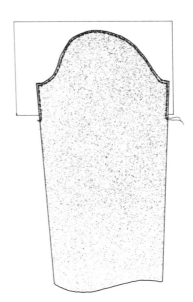

2. Trim the excess fabric around the sleeve cap. Turn over.

3. Cut and pin in place a patterned band right side up with both edges pressed under, overlapping the bottom of the top band.

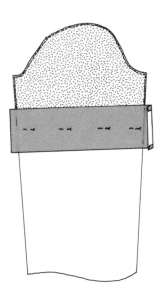

4. Cut a new piece of coordinated banding and slide its upper raw edge under the bottom edge of the patterned band.

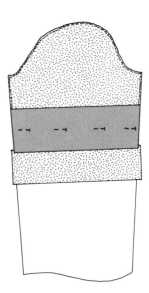

5. Cut two pieces of the piping you prepared about ½″ longer than the banding edges.

6. Slip the raw edges of the piping under the pressed edges of the patterned band and pin in place, the pins parallel to the piping with the heads in the direction shown in the illustration. This allows you to pull the pins out in front of the needle as you sew.

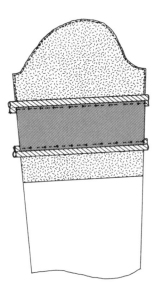

7. With a zipper foot sew the piping on the bands with the piping to the left of the foot.

8. Cover the entire sleeve with bands and piping by repeating steps 3 through 7.

Piped Appliqué

1. Cut the fronts and back of the jacket out of coordinated fabric.

2. Pin the fronts and backs to the lining fabrics, *wrong sides together.*

3. Staystitch around all outside edges.

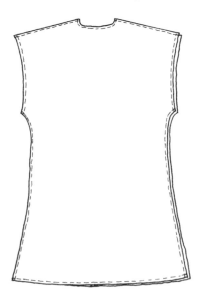

4. Pin your prepared appliqué shapes onto the front and back sections.

5. Slip piping under the edges of the shapes that will extend to the edge(s) of the garment pieces. Pin and sew the piping as in the bands on the sleeves (steps 6 and 7 of previous section).

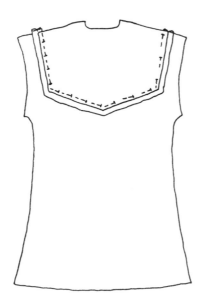

Applying Continuous Piped Appliqué

1. Pin piping around under the entire edge of an appliqué shape; cut the piping, allowing a 1″ overlap. Start stitching 1″ from one end of the piping and stop stitching 2″ from the other end.

2. Rip out the stitching on the "tailpiece" of the piping 1″. Fold back the piping fabric so it is clear of the scissors and trim the cording so both ends of it butt.

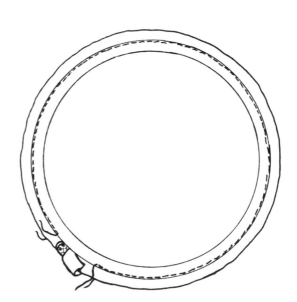

3. Smooth out the loose fabric; fold under one raw edge so that it covers the other raw end of the piping. Pin and stitch to complete appliqué of the motif.

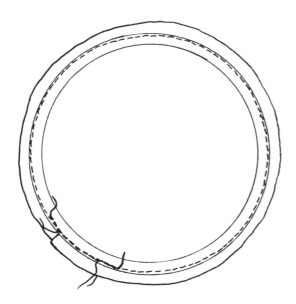

4. Continue in this manner until all motifs are appliquéd.

Jacket Construction

1. Sew shoulder seams on a sewing machine.

2. Clip excess cording out of the seam allowances.

ANN'S TIP. For greater ease in trimming, use a hemostat to hold cording. (See sources of supplies.)

---

3. If you have a serger, serge seam allowances together and press toward the jacket front. If you do not have a serger, zigzag the seam allowances or apply bias tape by hand to cover the raw edges.

4. Continue the jacket construction according to your pattern directions, finishing all seams as in steps 1 through 3 above.

CHAPTER SIX

Pickup Sticks Vest:
Ribbon Appliqué

MATERIAL

Vest pattern
Silk douppioni and thread to
    match
Lining
Ribbon
Tracing wheel and paper
Tear-off stabilizer
#1 noncorrosive safety pins
Nylon monofilament thread
Neutral thread

I made a black satin jacket with appliquéd ribbon parrots all over it for Offray, using tropical print ribbons. I crisscrossed the tropical ribbons all over the parrot motifs and stitched them down. It made a striking jacket: The black satin gave the jewel tones a dramatic setting.

I had scraps of leftover ribbons from the jacket, so I decided to use them as a vest. I chose to use black douppioni silk as a background fabric instead of black satin. Douppioni silk has nubby ridges woven into the cloth, giving it a wonderful texture and a subtle sheen. It is thick enough to be opaque and heavy enough to be easy to sew.

Choosing a Pattern

Choose any vest pattern from a commercial pattern book. The pattern can have darts or not. A darted pattern will fit the body better because it is less "boxy."

Preparation and Appliqué

1. Cut out the silk 1" larger all around than the pattern pieces. Mark all the darts on the wrong side of the fabric with tracing paper and a wheel.

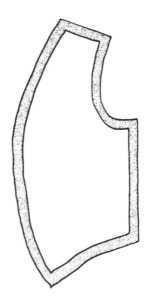

2. Silk douppioni does ravel after it has been cut. To prevent this either zigzag loose stitches around the outside edge or serge around the cut edges.

3. Cut pieces of tear-off stabilizer larger than the cut-out pattern pieces. Use #1 (1″) noncorrosive safety pins to pin the cut-out vest parts to the tear-off stabilizer.

4. To secure the fabric to the stabilizer, straight stitch all around the vest parts about ⅛″ from the cut edge. Start stitching about 2″ from an outside corner. This will correct any tucks that may form if the fabric shifts.

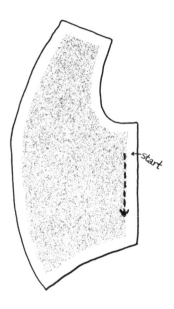

5. Thread your sewing machine with nylon monofilament thread on the top and a neutral thread in the bobbin.

6. Sew one ribbon diagonally across each of the sections.

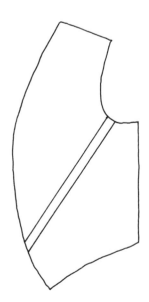

7. Sew each side of the ribbon in the same direction. Sew very close to the edge of the ribbon. Sewing in opposite directions may cause the ribbon to pucker. Sew ⅛"-wide ribbon down the center, not down each edge. Continue sewing ribbons all over the vest sections in different directions.

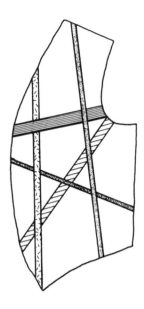

8. Tear off stabilizer from the back of the vest pieces. I recommend surgical hemostats to pull off small sections of stabilizer. They are easier to use than tweezers. (See Sources of Supplies).

9. Place your pattern pieces back onto the vest pieces and recut the garment to the actual size of the pattern.

ANN'S TIP. Use pattern weights instead of pins, and a rotary cutter and mat instead of scissors.

---

10. Cut out the lining of the vest. Mark the darts on the wrong side.

Vest Construction

1. Pin and sew all marked darts on both the vest sections and the linings. Press all darts to center or bottom.

ANN'S TIP. For double-pointed darts, you can split the sewn dart and press the seams open.

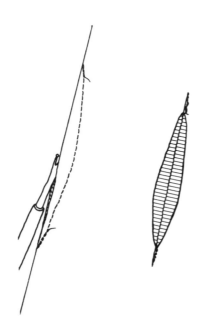

An alternate method is to clip the sewn dart to the seam line in several places and press it toward center of garment.

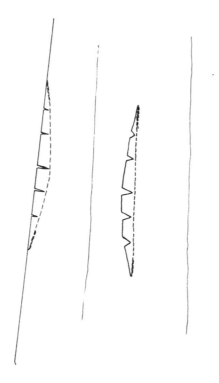

51

2. Right sides together, sew or serge all shoulder seams on the vest and lining. Press seams open (if you sewed) or toward the front (if you serged).

3. Lay out the vest lining, right side up.

4. Place the vest on top of the lining wrong side up (with the vest and lining right sides together).

5. Pin the lining and vest together around the entire vest, except the side seams.

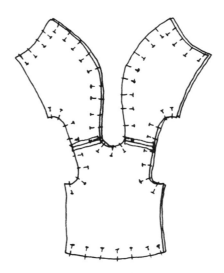

6. Sew or serge around all pinned seams but leave the side seams open. If you serged, go to step 8.

7. If you sewed, clip all curves and cut off outside corners.

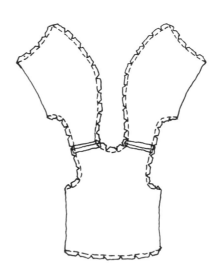

8. Reach through the back side seam opening, through the shoulder, and turn the vest fronts to the right side.

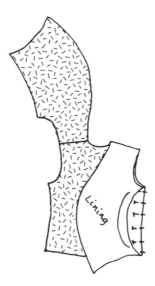

9. Press the vest around all sewn edges.

ANN'S TIP. Lay the vest face down on the ironing board for better control in pressing. This way you can be sure the lining won't show when you wear the vest.

---

10. Pull apart the vest and lining at the side seams and, right sides together, pin ONLY the vest side seams together, being sure that the top and bottom are matched.

11. With the right sides together, pin the lining side seams together an inch or two from the top and bottom of the vest.

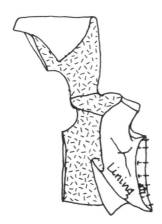

53

12. Keeping the lining edges free of the needle, start sewing the vest side seams of the pinned lining through the vest side seam, ending where the pins end in the lining at the other end, 1″ down from the side seam.

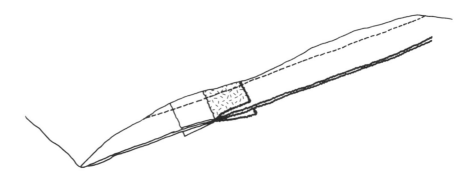

13. Carefully press open the vest side seams by holding the lining free of the iron. Try not to press the lining at this point. If the side seam is curved, clip the seam before you press it.

14. Press one edge of the lining along the seam line. (The pressed edge should lie on top of the unpressed lining, indicating where the seam is to be sewn.)

15. Hand sew the lining side seams.

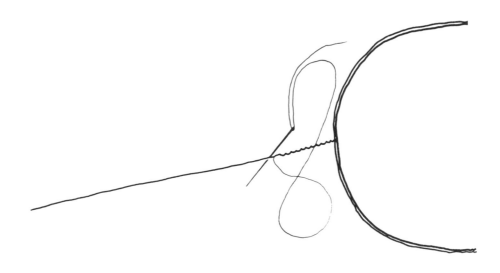

Satin-stitch appliqué gown, by author. Created with purchased appliqués.
Photos courtesy of Fairfield Processing

Pickup Sticks vest, by author. Straight-stitch appliqué with Offray Ribbons on douppioni (Ch. 6). *Photo by Mark Jenkins*

Crazy patchwork jacket, by author.
Patchwork of vintage metallic and brocade
fabrics, embellished with decorative stitches
and ribbon thread. *Photo by Mark Jenkins*

Leaf and Hogwash jackets, by author.
Satin-stitch appliqué leaf jacket (Ch. 8);
machine straight-stitch appliqué (Ch. 4).
Both created for Concord Fabrics. *Photos by
Mark Jenkins*

Southwestern vest, by author.
Stained-glass appliqué technique
(Ch. 7). *Photo by Mark Jenkins*

Oriental jacket, by author. Award-winning gold-piped appliqué jacket (Ch. 5); created for Concord Fabrics. *Photo by Mark Jenkins*

Aloha Diamond Head, by author.
Bomber jacket is appliquéd with
decorative stitches (Ch. 15); hat is
three-dimensional appliqué
(Ch. 10). *Photo courtesy of
Fairfield Processing*

CHAPTER SEVEN

Southwestern Vest:
Stained-Glass
Appliqué

MATERIALS

Vest pattern

Tissue lamé and matching
    thread

Muslin

Rotary cutter, Plexiglas ruler,
    and mat (optional)

Bias tape maker (optional)

Various textured fabrics for
    background

Long, thin, plastic flower-head
    pins (optional)

Rickrack

Rattail or rayon cord

Darning or circular foot

Cording foot

Ready-made sequin appliqués

Nylon monofilament thread

Neutral thread

I was working in a booth at a trade show when one of my friends rushed up to me and exclaimed that one of the vendors was selling off their sequin appliqués at wholesale at the close of the show. Of course, being bargain conscious, I rushed over and purchased a bunch of southwestern motifs. One was a howling coyote under a full moon, and my imagination immediately saw this motif on a dark blue background. In my collection of fabrics I found a range of cobalt blues, so I decided to make a vest with those blues as the background for the coyotes and cacti. My fabric stash yielded blue velvets, satins, moirés, and lamés, as well as metallic blue rickrack and rattail cord. These elements all came together in a vest made with my updated stained-glass appliqué technique.

The basis of stained-glass appliqué is to use bias tape to cover the raw fabric edges of the appliqués. Traditionally, stained-glass appliqué is made with black bias tape outlining jewel-tone fabrics in the background. The finished work resembles stained-glass windows. This project is an updated version of stained-glass appliqué, using bias-cut tissue lamé to replace the traditional black bias tape. I embellished the stained-glass background with ready-made sequined appliqués.

Making Bias Tape

The fabric used for the bias tape for this project is tissue lamé, a thin fabric that is woven with metallic and nylon fibers. It is extremely ravel-prone, but when it is cut on the bias it will not ravel.

1. Cut up your tissue lamé fabric into bias strips at a 45° angle. I used ½"-wide bias tape, so I cut 1"-wide strips. Allow ¼"

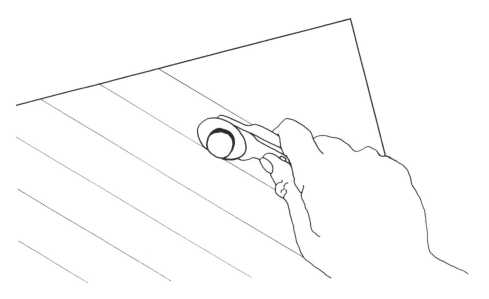

on each side to turn under the raw edges, adding that total ½″ to the finished width you desire. A rotary cutter, Plexiglas ruler, and mat with a 45°-angle grid printed on it are ideal tools for this step.

2. Sew the strips right sides together end-to-end in a continuous strip. When you pin two diagonal edges together in a "V", the two outside tips should extend ¼″ on either side. These tips are called "dog ears".

As shown below, you can sew the strips together in a chain method. Sew the first two ends together and stitch a short thread chain. Without cutting the thread, sew together the other end of one of the first strips and a third strip. Continue in this way until all of the strips are joined and then snip the thread chains in between the seams.

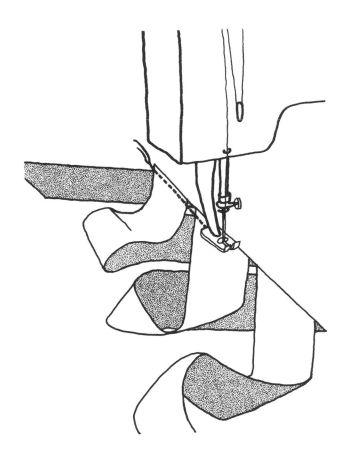

3. Press the seams open. Tissue lamé can be ironed directly with no pressing cloth. Be sure to lower the iron's heat to the silk setting and move the iron quickly. Too much heat will cause the lamé to crinkle and/or melt.

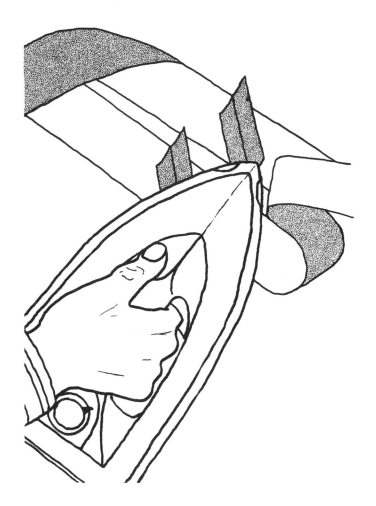

4. Trim off the "dog ears".

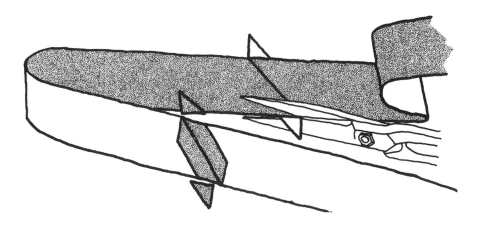

5. With a bias tape maker and an iron, make one continuous bias strip. Bias tape makers come in ½″, 1″, 1½″, and 2″ widths. (Instructions for an alternative method follow.)

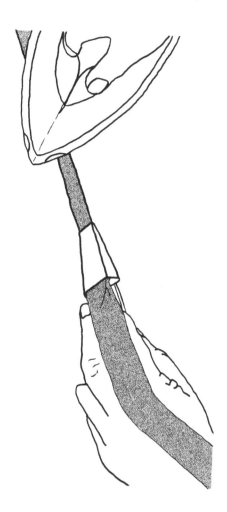

6. Roll the bias tape into a tube and secure it with a pin.

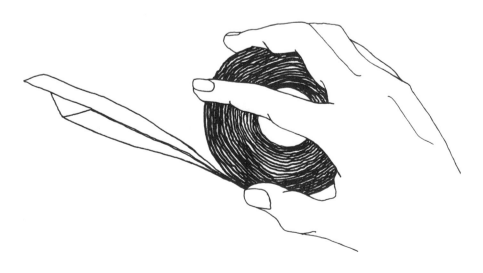

Here is an alternative to making bias strips with bias tape makers. The alternative allows unlimited width variations.

1. To determine the width of fabric to cut for bias strips, double the width you need and add double seam allowances. For example, if you want a strip ⅞″ wide, cut your bias strips 2¼″ wide (⅞″ + ⅞″ + ¼″ + ¼″). Fold the strip(s) in half lengthwise, *wrong* sides together.

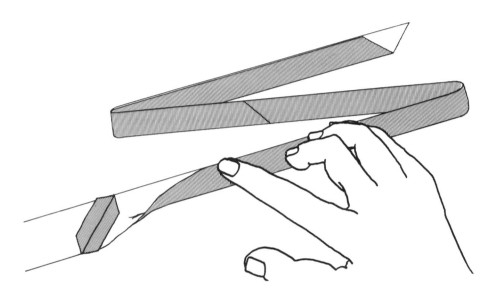

2. Stitch along raw edges at your seam allowance. (You may want to trim your seam allowance to ⅛″.) Press the strip flat with the raw edge concealed on the center of the underside.

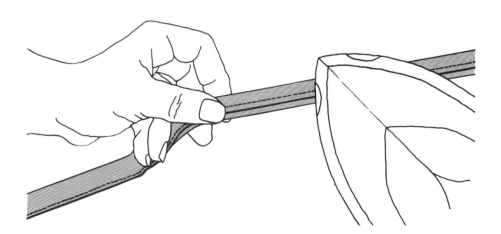

ANN'S TIP. Metal bars for this method (available by mail) can be inserted into the strips for less fussy, more accurate pressing.

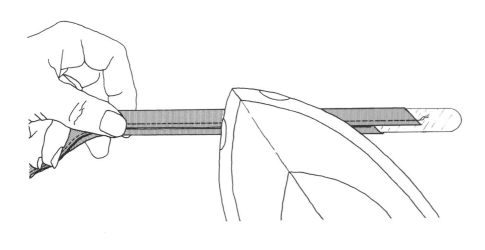

ANN'S TIP. To facilitate sewing small seam allowances over the feed dogs, you may find it helpful to sew with a narrow strip of typing paper or tearaway stabilizer under your fabric.

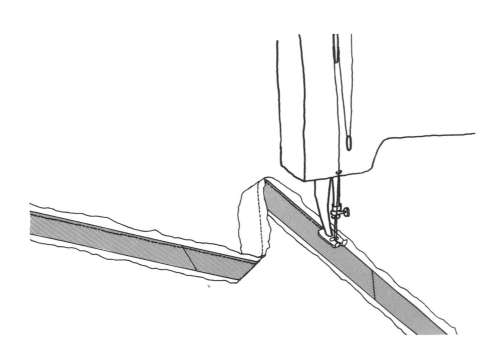

Choosing a Pattern

Choose any vest pattern from a commercial pattern book. The pattern can have darts or not. A darted pattern will fit the body better because it will be less "boxy." I lined my vest.

Layering the Background Fabrics

The background fabrics have a mixture of textures. They are topstitched onto a muslin base with their raw edges butted and left exposed. These raw edges are later covered with the tissue lamé bias tape.

1. Adding 1″ all around, cut out the pattern pieces in muslin.

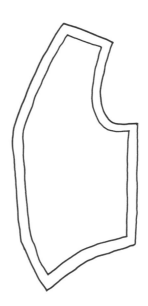

2. Begin at the bottom of the vest. Lay a piece of background fabric right side down on your table. This fabric can be of any size, the only requirement being that it extend at least from side-to-side of the muslin garment piece. Lay the muslin, right side down, on top of the background fabric. Pin the fabrics in place. With wrong sides still up, stitch very close to the muslin, as shown. Use a longer stitch length (6–8 to the inch or 4.0–4.5) for this step and you will reduce puckering of the fabric.

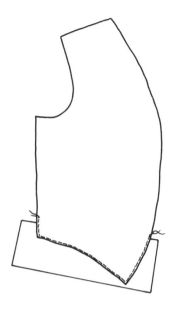

3. Trim off the excess background fabric around the muslin.

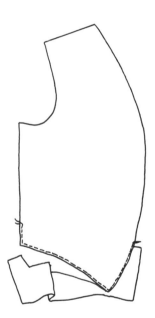

4. Flip the vest section to its right side. Pin another type of background fabric, right side up, on top of the muslin, overlapping the previous background fabric about 2″.

5. Sew a curved line across the garment section, catching all three layers of fabric (muslin, first background, and second background).

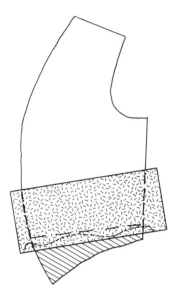

6. Trim off the background fabric below the curved stitching line very close to the stitches.

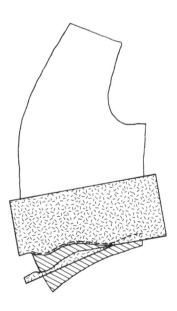

7. Flip the vest section again so the wrong side is up and stitch the second background piece along the outside edges of the muslin.

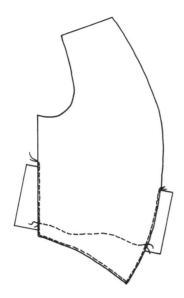

8. Trim any excess fabric.

9. Repeat steps 4 through 8 until the entire garment section is covered.

Applying Bias Strips and Trims

1. Pin the bias tape you've prepared across all of the topstitched seams, centering the raw edges of the background fabrics under the bias tape.

2. Topstitch each edge of the bias tape with matching thread. I used blue metallic thread on blue bias. Stitch each edge of the bias tape in the same direction. Sewing in opposite directions will cause puckering.

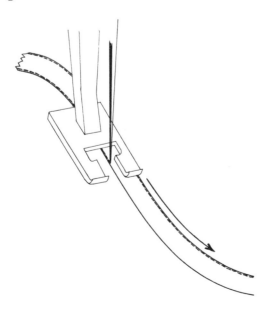

3. Topstitch parallel rows of rickrack to decorate some of the sections.

4. Rattail or rayon cord is easily sewn with a cording foot in a swiggle or continuous "S" on some sections. The cord will tunnel under the foot while you loosely zigzag over it, couching it onto the background fabric. Set the width of the zigzag wide enough to clear both edges of the cord.

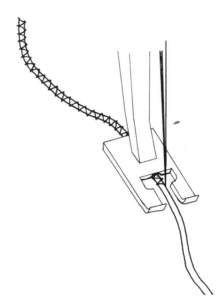

Vest Construction

1. Pin and sew all marked darts on both the vest sections and the linings. Press all darts to the center or bottom. For double-pointed darts split the sewn dart and press the seams open.

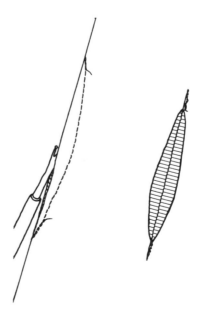

An alternate method, which works just as well, is to clip the sewn dart to the seamline in several places and press it toward the center of the garment.

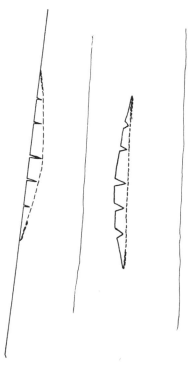

2. Right sides together, sew or serge all shoulder seams on both the vest and lining. Press the seams open (if you sewed) or toward the front (if you serged).

3. Lay open the vest lining right side up.

4. Place the outer vest wrong side up on top of the lining (so the vest and lining are right sides together).

5. Pin the lining and vest together around the entire vest, except the side seams.

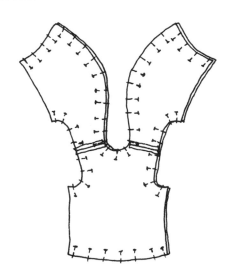

6. Sew or serge around all of the pinned seams but leave the side seams open. If you serged, go to step 8.

7. If you sewed, clip all of the curves and cut off the outside corners.

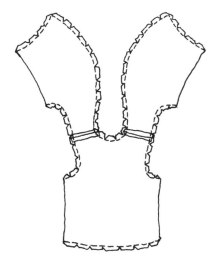

8. Reach through the back side seam opening, through the shoulder seam, and turn the vest fronts to the right side.

9. Press the vest around all sewn edges.

ANN'S TIP. Lay the vest face down on the ironing board for better control in pressing: this way you can be sure the lining won't show when you wear the vest.

---

10. Pull apart the vest and lining at the side seams and, right sides together, pin ONLY the vest side seams together, being sure that the top and bottom are matched.

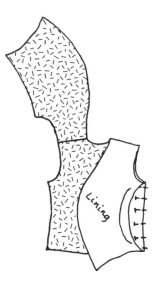

11. Right sides together, pin the lining side seams together an inch or two from the top and bottom of the vest.

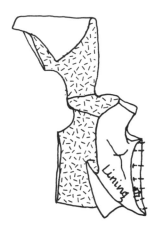

ANN'S TIP. Use the free arm on the machine for side seam sewing.

---

12. Keeping the lining edges free of the needle, start sewing vest side seams from the pinned lining through the vest side seam, ending where the pins end in the lining at the other end.

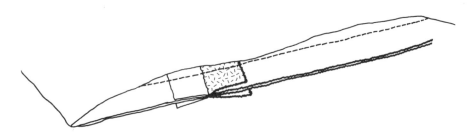

13. Carefully press open the vest side seams by holding the lining free of the iron. If the side seam is curved, clip seams before you press.

14. Press one edge of the lining along seam line. (The pressed edge should lie on top of the unpressed lining, indicating where the seam is to be sewn.)

15. Hand sew the lining side seams.

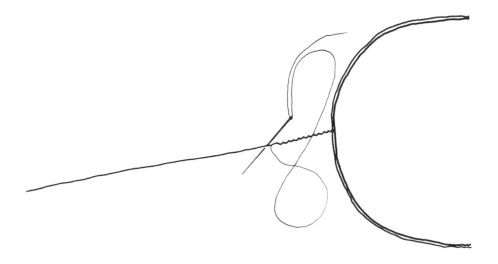

Applying Sequin Appliqués

1. Carefully pin each of the appliqués onto the finished vest with two or three straight pins. A longer, thin, plastic flower-headed pin works best.

ANN'S TIP. Instead of pins, you can use Clotilde/Aleene's sticky reusable glue: spray it on the wrong side of the appliqué and finger press it into place.

---

2. Put a darning or circular foot on the sewing machine.

ANN'S TIP. Schmetz manufactures a needle with a built-on spring that will substitute for a sewing machine foot.

---

3. Lower the feed dogs. Thread the machine with monofilament thread and thread the bobbin with a neutral thread.

4. Carefully stitch, one stitch at a time, just inside the edge of a sequin appliqué. Be careful to stitch between the sequins and beads. If you inadvertently sew through a sequin, it will not split, but it will leave a hole.

ANN'S TIP. An alternative to sewing on the sequin appliqués is to use a removable adhesive spray, like Sticky Stuff from Clotilde (see Sources of Supplies). The motif can then be removed and repositioned. Spray the product on the back of the appliqué and place it where you want it on the garment.

---

5. Attach all sequin motifs as desired. Never iron or press near or behind a sequin motif because heat dulls the colors of the sequins.

PART THREE

SATIN-STITCH APPLIQUÉ

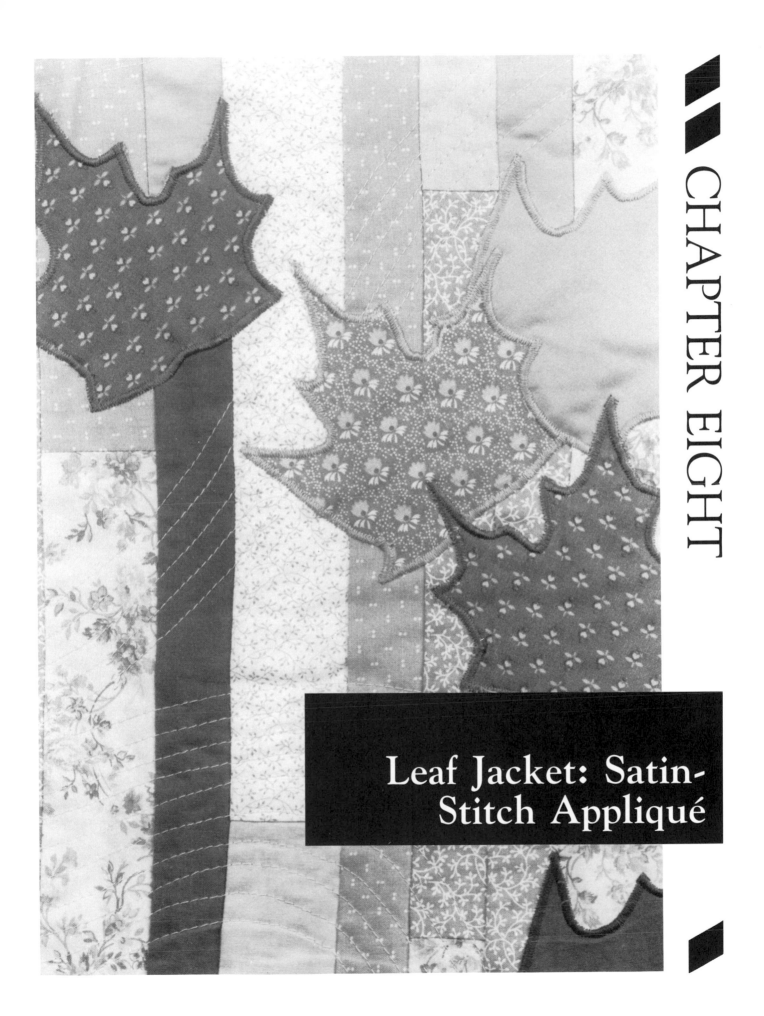

CHAPTER EIGHT

Leaf Jacket: Satin-Stitch Appliqué

Several years ago, Concord Fabrics called me when one of its long-term employees was retiring from the company. I was commissioned to make a friendship quilt incorporating muslin squares which Concord employees had autographed. Concord sent me fabrics in coordinating earth tones—perfect for a quilt for this man. I made strip-pieced patchwork, which I cut into 10″ blocks. I decided to machine appliqué some leaves all over the quilt. Instead of throwing the scraps away, I later sewed the leftover fabrics and leaves into a jacket for me. I sewed a "Concord Fabrics" logo strip into the jacket to make it a "designer" quilted jacket version of "Alligator" shirts.

This garment project combines satin-stitch appliqué and staggered strip-piecing patchwork. The actual appliqué process requires no fusing or other preparation. The batting beneath the patchwork substitutes as a machine-quilting technique. The finished jacket will not have the stiffness that is common in conventional fused appliqué.

Choosing a Pattern and Fabrics

Choose a commercial jacket pattern that has large sections with no darts. A pattern with one back, two fronts and two sleeves is easiest. A shawl collar and cuffs in contrasting fabric set off the patchwork and appliqué nicely.

ANN'S TIP. An unlined pattern is easily converted to a lined jacket: The outer pattern pieces are cut out of the lining fabric and sewn according to the pattern directions. Then the lining and the constructed quilted jacket are combined to complete the garment. To eliminate bulk, cut the linings off at the folded hem edge so that the facings and hems are turned onto the lining. If the pattern has facings, use them.

You will need approximately 1 to 1½ yards more fabric than the specified yardage requirements on the pattern directions. For example, a jacket that uses 3¼ yards needs about 4½ yards of fabric.

MATERIALS

Jacket pattern

Fabric scraps, 6–12 colors, for patchwork

Contrasting fabric scraps for leaf appliqués

Thread to match

Lining

Batting

Rotary cutter, Plexiglas ruler, and mat (optional)

#1 noncorrosive safety pins

Even feed or walking foot

Template material (acetate)

Grease pencil

Paper scissors

Silver Berol pencil

Appliqué foot

Shoulder pads

Embroidery scissors

ANN'S TIP. A quilter can use leftover fabric strips from quilt projects, such as log-cabin quilts. This is an economical use of fabric strips.

Choose between six and twelve colors for the patchwork. These colors can be monochromatic (shades of one color) or a variety of different colors. The leaf pattern is used for the appliqué over the patchwork. Either scraps or small yardages may be used for the leaves. Choose for the leaves fabrics that are not in your patchwork, so as to gain high contrast between background and leaves.

Earth or autumn colors will make the jacket look more natural. The jacket is a garment, so choose colors that are attractive on the person who will be wearing it, rather than just artistic color choices.

Cutting and Joining Strips

1. Fold your fabric for patchwork in half, with the selvages together. If you are using scraps without selvages, fold the fabric on the straight grain.

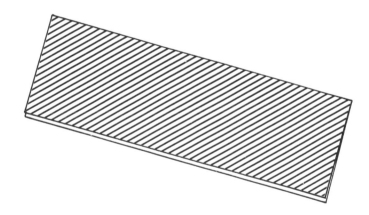

2. Fold this folded fabric in half again so there are now four thicknesses.

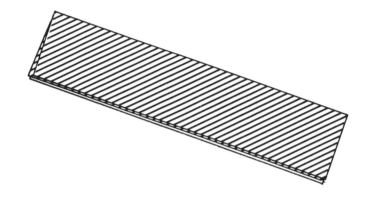

3. Using a rotary cutter, mat, and Plexiglas ruler, square the bottom raw edges. Cut up all your yardage into strips of two different widths, 1½″ and 2″. Be sure to cut strips on the straight grain.

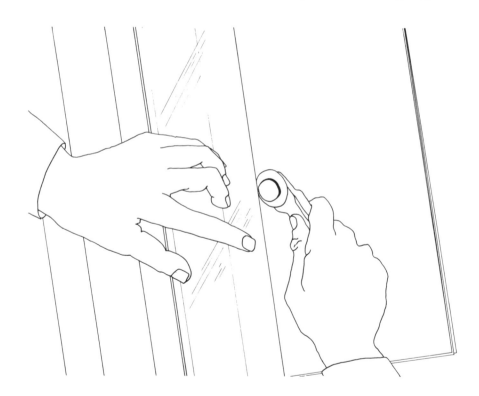

4. Repeat steps 1 through 3 for all of your patchwork fabrics.

5. Cut the strips into lengths, varying between 4″ and 18″.

6. Using a ¼″ seam allowance, sew the strips right sides together end-to-end with a "chain" method. Always join two unlike strips.

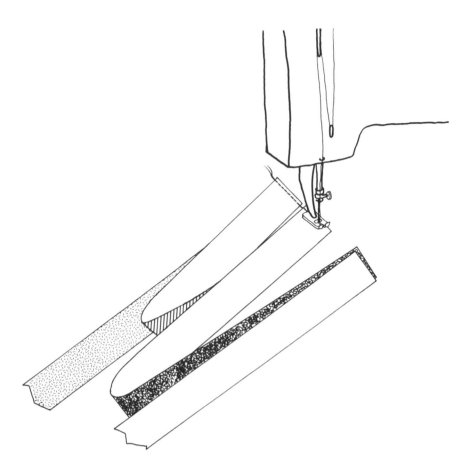

7. Clip chain sewing apart, creating one very long strip. Press the seams to one side and roll up the strip as you iron. Secure the end with a straight pin.

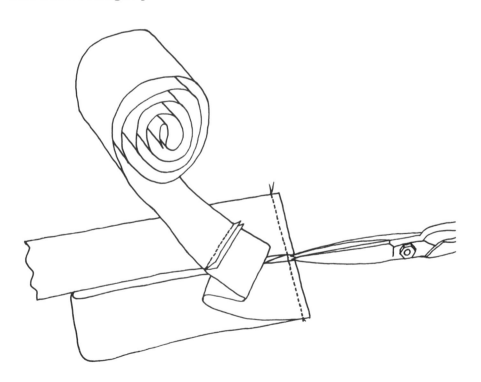

Sewing Strips Together to Create Patchwork

1. Measure the length of a pattern piece at the longest vertical dimension (e.g., sleeve cap to wrist, center back to hem) and cut from your rolled strip a length 2″ longer. Using that strip as a guide, cut a second strip the same length (or longer if any of your cross seams match—seams must always be staggered).

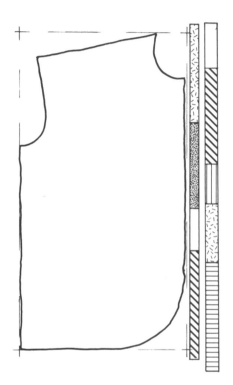

2. Sew or serge these two strips together lengthwise, right sides together. Continue joining strips until the patchwork piece is 2″ wider than the pattern piece.

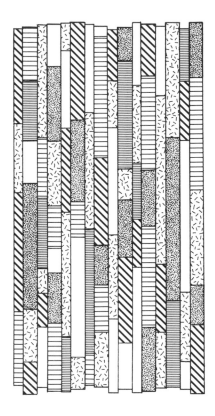

3. Press all seams in one direction.

4. Repeat this process for all of the pattern pieces. You should have a patchwork piece for the back; two pieces for the fronts; two pieces for the sleeves.

Cutting Out and Layering

1. Pin each appropriate pattern piece onto its patchwork and cut out around the pattern edge about 1″ larger than the pattern edge, just "eyeballing" the extra allowance as you cut. **Note:** Be sure to reverse the pattern front and sleeve so you have left and right pieces.

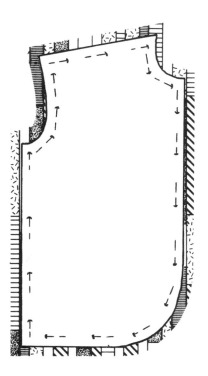

2. Lay each patchwork section onto a piece of batting and cut out the batting 1″ larger all around the patchwork section.

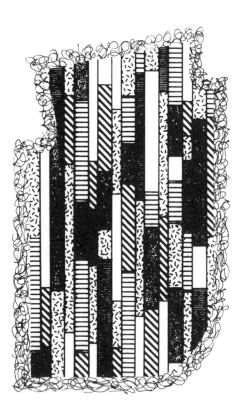

ANN'S TIP. Fairfield Processing's Cotton Classic batting can be split in half for a softer, more drapable garment. To split Cotton Classic batting, pull apart one corner, separating the batting until there are two halves.

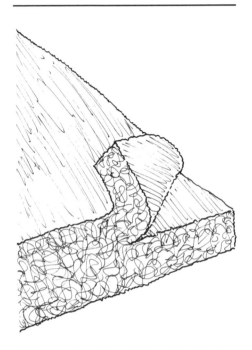

Place the soft (center) side of the split batting against the wrong side of the patchwork.

3. Pin-baste each patchwork section onto the batting pieces, using #1 (1″) noncorrosive safety pins. Pin every 6″ to secure patchwork to batting.

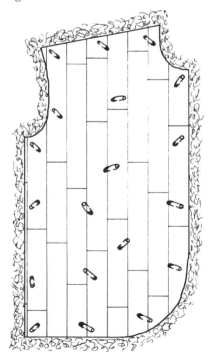

ANN'S TIP. Although I buy these noncorrosive safety pins wholesale by the industrial size box (12 gross), large quantities of safety pins are available either in shops or by mail order (see Sources of Supplies). Always store safety pins in an open position for later use. If you have a smaller amount of pins, dedicate a pincushion to them.

Machine Quilting the Layers

1. Put an even feed or walking foot onto your sewing machine, or if you have a Pfaff, engage the built-in dual feed (see Sources).

2. Thread your sewing machine with a neutral color of thread that coordinates with the patchwork colors.

3. Set the stitch length to 3.5–4.0 length, or about 8 stitches to the inch.

4. Sew a curved line through the center of the patchwork. Use a reverse stitch to lock stitches at both the beginning and the end of the line.

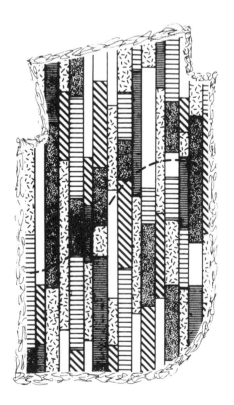

ANN'S TIP. If you need a guideline, mark it with a leftover sliver of a white soap bar. This can be brushed off later. Or use a chalk marker pencil or wheel, which can also be brushed off later.

---

5. Use the right-hand side of the sewing machine foot as your guide to sew another line parallel to the first. Repeat this to form three or five lines. See step 7 to determine how far apart you want the lines. I don't really plan ahead, but quilt freely.

6. Begin at another point and sew another quilting line. Repeat step 5.

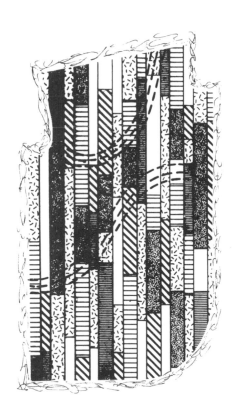

7. Continue sewing parallel quilting lines all over the patchwork. There can be unquilted areas as large as six square inches. (Appliquéd leaves will later cover these sections.) Remove safety pins as you sew.

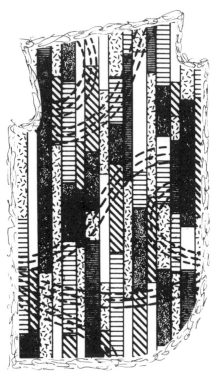

ANN'S TIP. **If you need to fill up a small section, sew a continuous curve, using a ceramic or plastic dinner plate, lunch plate, or saucer as a pattern.**

8. If a stitching line begins or ends in the center of the patchwork, the stitches need to be secured. If you have a lockstitch button, use it. Lacking the lockstitch, draw up the bobbin thread either by tapping the pedal or by manually turning the flywheel. Then sew several stitches in one place. Lower or cover the feed dogs or set the stitch length to zero.

ANN'S TIP. **For a fast lockstitch, leave the feed dogs up and don't change the machine settings. Hold the fabric with your hands so it can't move and sew about six stitches in place. Release the fabric and continue sewing. Repeat this process for ending stitches.**

Cutwork appliqué ensemble by
Jennifer Amor. *Photo courtesy
of Fairfield Processing*

Shadow appliqué, by Toby Davidson.
Collar using shadow technique (Ch. 14).
*Courtesy of Toby O Creations; photo by
Mark Jenkins*

Clamshell quilt, by author. Invisible appliqué; created for J&P Coats. *Photo courtesy of Grass Roots Publishing*

Hawaiian Snowflake quilt, by author. Satin-stitch appliqué and machine echo quilting; created for J&P Coats. *Photo courtesy of Grass Roots Publishing*

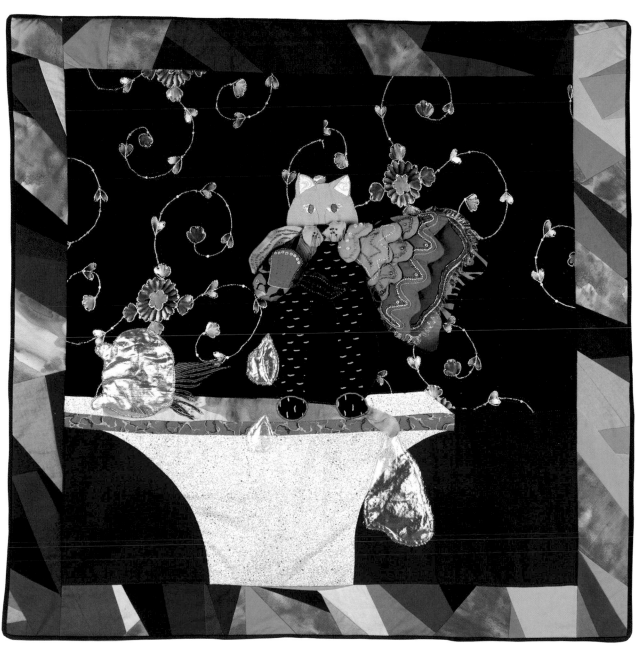

Catch of the Day, by Charlotte Angotti. Appliqué over stuffing and other appliqué techniques. *Courtesy of the artist; photo by Mark Jenkins*

Satin-stitch appliqué, by author. Created for Alexander Henry. *Photo courtesy of Grass Roots Publishing*

Preparing the Motifs

1. Trace the full-size leaf templates at the end of this chapter onto a piece of thin plastic with a grease pencil. (Paper or cardboard will deteriorate.) A free source of plastic is a used x-ray sheet. These are usually thrown out at medical centers. Beg or borrow them from someone who works at one. Clear acetate is sold in art and toy stores. Quilt stores carry acetate with a grid printed on it, but this is more expensive. You can draw on this plastic with a lead pencil. Cut out the templates with paper scissors, not your good fabric shears.

2. Layer four different fabrics. Trace leaf patterns onto the top layer. Use a Berol silver pencil, available in art and quilt stores, not a pen. From this point, handle the four layers as one and you will save time cutting. There is no need to pin the fabric together, and the pin may distort your appliqués.

3. Cut out the leaf shape on the drawn line, holding the fabric together with your hand.

4. Pin the leaves around your patchwork in an attractive manner. Use one #1 safety pin to secure each leaf. They can be overlapped in twos and threes, as well as singly. Do not pin leaves too close to outside edges.

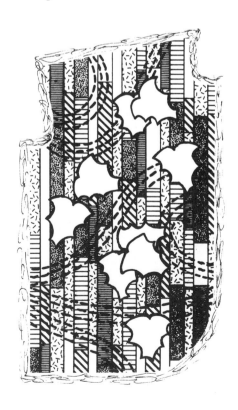

ANN'S TIP. Use the reverse (wrong) side of fabrics for a subtle color change.

Appliquéing the Leaves

1. Choose threads that match your leaves.

2. Thread your sewing machine with thread that matches one of the underneath leaves. (Multilayered appliqué is always sewn from the bottom shape upward.) If a bobbin thread shows on the front, match your bobbin thread to the top thread color.

ANN'S TIP. On a Bernina, thread the bobbin thread through the hole on the finger on the bobbin case. This will keep the bobbin thread from showing on the top stitches. Then your bobbin thread color will not need to be changed with each change of top color.

---

3. Attach an appliqué foot to the machine. This type of foot has a groove underneath which allows the bulky satin stitch to keep moving through the machine. If there is a choice of feet, use the foot with the best visibility. An open toe appliqué foot has the best visibility. This will work well with the thickness of the batting and fabrics in this project; but on a thinner project, the fabric will tunnel between the toes of the foot. This will result in puckered appliqué. To adapt a regular appliqué foot into an open toe foot, cut off the front bar and file it smooth (or, if the foot is plastic, snap it off with needle-nose pliers).

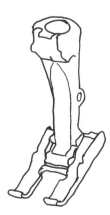

4. Lower the upper tension slightly.

5. Set your machine to a medium width zigzag stitch.

6. Set your machine to a short stitch length using one of these methods, depending on what machine you use. Set your machine at 6 o'clock on a mechanical model of Bernina:

On some machines, you'll use the setting below the #1 stitch length; halfway in the buttonhole setting of some other machines; or .35 or 0.5 on newer computer machines. Always test stitch on a scrap first.

7. Draw up the bobbin thread. There is no need to lockstitch.

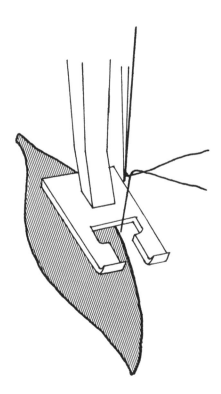

8. Begin stitching at any point of the leaf design with the right swing of the needle just off the right raw edge of the appliqué. The left swing of the needle is in the appliqué.

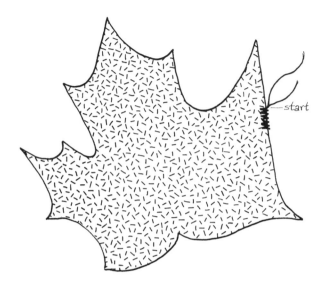

9. Satin stitch around the entire leaf motif in a clockwise direction, then lockstitch.

To appliqué outside points:

1. Sew up to a point as far as the zigzag width permits.

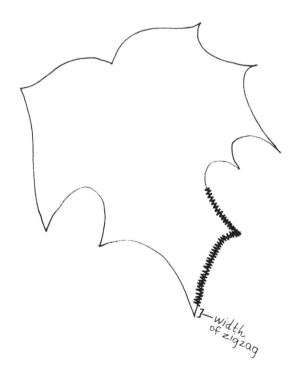

2. Stop with the needle in the outer (background) fabric.

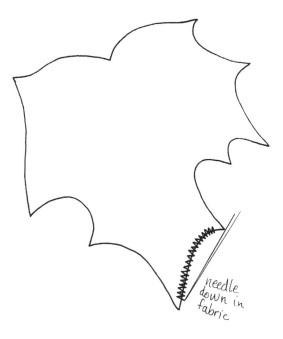

needle
down in
fabric

3. On a machine that will gradually dial a narrow width, slowly move the dial and sew at the same time until the needle is at the outside point. Leave the needle in the fabric.

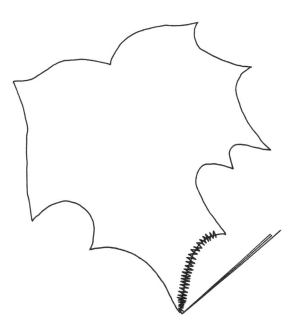

Satin-Stitch Appliqué

If your machine has separate width settings, you will have a stairstep effect with this method.

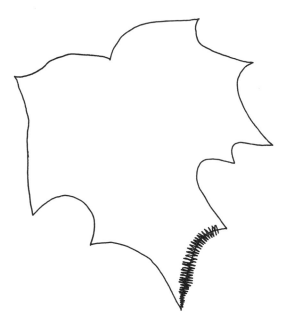

To remedy this stairstep effect:

• Satin stitch toward the point until the distance to the point equals the width of the zigzag.

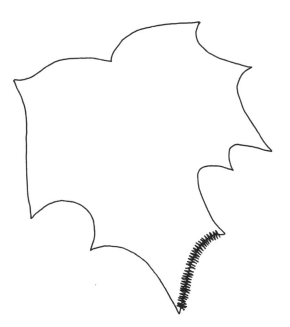

• Leave the needle in the background fabric and turn the fabric so the swing of the needle is parallel to the edge of the appliqué. Sew very slowly (or use the hand wheel) to create a "fan" by spreading the stitches on the left of the zigzag, but always returning the needle to the appliqué point. End the "fan" with the needle on the left swing (in the background fabric).

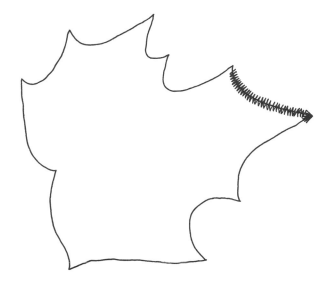

• Turn the fabric and continue to satin stitch away from the point.

To appliqué inside points:

1. Zigzag into the inside point. Leave the needle in the appliqué fabric.

2. Lift the presser foot and turn the fabric counterclockwise.

3. Readjust the needle so that the right swing of the needle will be both at the sewn zigzag stitches and the upcoming right raw edge of the fabric.

To satin-stitch curves:

1. When the fabric starts to curve, stop with the needle in the fabric (either swing direction).

2. Lift the presser foot and turn the fabric clockwise slightly.

ANN'S TIP. Most Bernina machines have a knee-lift bar for the presser foot that will free both your hands for turning.

3. Lower the presser foot and sew a few more stitches. Repeat this process until the curve is sewn.

ANN'S TIP. To eliminate lifting the presser foot while sewing curves, press the edge of the appliqué with the fingers of your left hand, and place your right-hand fingers parallel to the left on the background fabric. Maintaining constant pressure from both hands, turn your work counterclockwise, feeding it into the needle. Work the fingers close to the presser foot to avoid puckering the appliqué fabric.

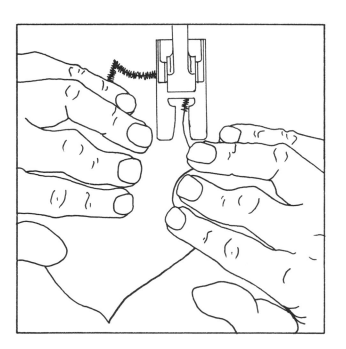

Finishing the Garment Sections

1. Cut out the fabric for the collar and cuffs 1″ larger all around than the pattern pieces.

2. Pin these pieces onto batting with #1 safety pins. Cut out the batting 1″ larger in all dimensions than the collar and cuffs.

3. Machine quilt parallel free-form lines on these sections. Use the width of the presser foot as a guide.

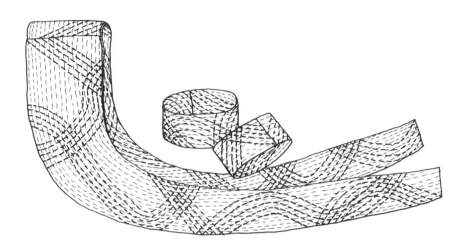

4. Pin each pattern piece onto each section and recut the quilted section to the actual size of the pattern. Be sure to mark the notches on the pattern. Note: *Be sure to flip-flop the front and sleeve pattern pieces to get a left and a right of each.* Sew together the shoulder seams on the sewing machine.

5. Using sharp embroidery scissors, carefully cut away the excess batting in the seam allowances.

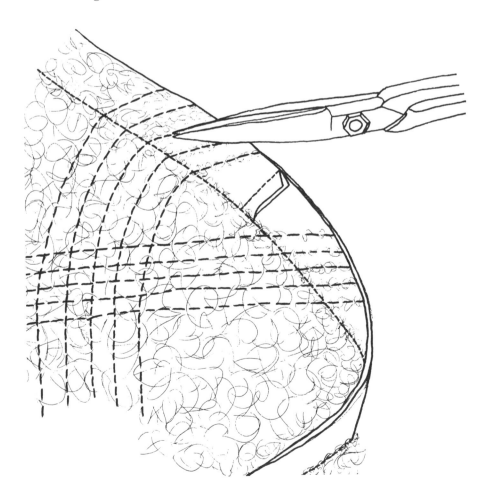

6. Either press open the seams or serge the edges. Then sew the sleeves onto the body as specified in the pattern directions. Trim and press. Sew the sleeve and jacket side seams. Trim and press. Sew the collar and cuff sections onto the jacket. Trim and press.

Making the Lining

1. Cut out the lining following the pattern instructions. If you've chosen an unlined garment pattern, cut out the same pattern sections as you did for the appliquéd patchwork (back, sleeves and fronts).

ANN'S TIP. Cut the lining out of a cotton print to coordinate with the jacket. It will wear better than a conventional lining, particularly with a quilted jacket.

---

2. Sew shoulder pads onto the batting side of the jacket shoulders *or* cover shoulder pads and tack them into the finished jacket after completion.

3. Sew or serge together the lining. Press open the seams if you sewed.

4. Turn under and press the hemline. Press the raw edge of the collar and front edges along the seam line toward the inside. Press the raw edge of the cuffs toward the sleeves. Where necessary, clip the seam allowance so it will lie flat.

5. Slip the lining into the jacket sleeves. Hand-stitch the lining onto the turned-under jacket edges. Trim any excess turned-in fabric to reduce bulk.

6. Machine topstitch around the edges of the collar, front, and cuffs. Topstitch five parallel rows using the edge of the presser foot as a width gauge.

CHAPTER NINE

Cutwork

Years ago I had to sew up a magazine project using cutwork appliqué. Although I had a general knowledge of the technique, I needed to work through many technical problems.

The first project I attempted used a satin-stitch method throughout: The design was satin stitched and then the background was cut away. The problem with this technique is that no matter how carefully you cut the fabric away from the edge of the satin stitches, there will still be fiber "whiskers" on the cut edge. In short, this technique looks sloppy. The best-looking technique for cutwork is to cut away the background first and then satin stitch over the cut edges—the method described in this chapter.

Transfering a Pattern to Fabric

Cutwork appliqué is generally a "connect-the-dots" method of sewing. The patterns are usually floral, but there are in any case two design considerations: The motifs must touch each other physically; and there must be positive/negative contrast. Patterns can be found in books in libraries and mail-order catalogs, such as Aardvark and Clotilde (see Sources of Supplies).

The easiest way to transfer a pattern is to use a water-soluble stabilizer product (see Sources of Supplies) and a wash-out blue pen. A pencil may tear the Solvy or pull it out of shape. Solvy is such a see-through film. Pin it loosely on top of the cutwork fabric

MATERIALS

Cutwork pattern
Water-soluble stabilizer
Fusible, tear-off, or liquid stabilizer
Wash-out blue pen
Fabric
Contrasting thread
Lightbox (optional)
Darning, open-embroidery, or spring foot
Embroidery scissors

with your cutwork pattern sandwiched in between. Trace the pattern and then move the pattern to its next location and trace it again.

You can trace or draw a design directly onto the fabric if you prefer, but be forewarned that it can be hard to do. If the fabric is light enough in color, you may be able to place the pattern beneath the fabric and see through it to trace the pattern onto the fabric.

ANN'S TIP. Use a lightbox to help you see a pattern under your fabric for easy pattern transferring. A no-cost substitute is to tape the pattern and fabric to a sunny window.

Depending on the stabilizer you choose from the methods below, you will need to stabilize the wrong side of the fabric before or after transferring the pattern. This will eliminate the need for a cumbersome embroidery hoop. It will also give needed stiffness or body to the fabric, helping to minimize puckered stitches.

There are several methods to stabilize the fabric. A permanent solution is to fuse a 100% woven cotton interfacing or a fusible knit interfacing **before** the design is transferred. Alternatively, pin a tear-off stabilizer underneath the project. Sulky makes an iron-on tear-away stabilizer called "Totally Stable." This product will eliminate shifting, sliding, and puckering. The excess stabilizer tears away easily, leaving no sticky residue. You will want to adhere this stabilizer **before** you transfer the design. A fourth stabilizer is Palmer/Pletsch's "Perfect Sew," a liquid stabilizer that is painted onto the fabric. After the fabric is dry, iron it to remove wrinkles and firm the fabric, and then transfer the cutwork design. After you have sewn the fabric, rinse it in warm running water to remove Perfect Sew.

Sewing Cutwork Appliqué

The easiest method for the first step is to set up the sewing machine for free-motion sewing. Lower the feed dogs or cover them with a separate plate. Most machines have a button or knob which will lower the feed dogs. Next, install a darning foot, open-embroidery foot, or spring foot.

ANN'S TIP. On some machines, particularly Viking/Husqvarna, dial the presser-foot dial to the "darning" motif. It looks like a "#" at the botton of the numbers.

ANN'S TIP. On a newer Pfaff there are three levels on the presser-foot handle. The middle level is for free-motion work.

---

1. Before you sew, you must always lower the presser-foot lever since this engages the top tension.

The fabric between the sewing-machine foot and the feed dogs should be able to move around freely. Some machines don't have much room for fabric when the feed dogs are covered with a separate plate and the appropriate foot is attached. If that is your situation, remove the cover plate: Even with the feed dogs exposed, you can still sew free-motion. On most machines set the stitch length to 0 to minimize wear and tear on the feed dogs. They still move on higher stitch length settings even when they are dropped.

2. Sew cutwork appliqué with a contrasting thread color, traditionally one or two shades darker than the fabric. A Fairfield Fashion Show garment in black-and-white cutwork was made by Jennifer Amor of Columbia, S.C. As a lining behind the cutwork embroidery, she used opposite colors of fabric. My cutwork project with the daisy pattern is sewn with the traditional method of a darker shade of thread on a lighter color fabric. I personally choose my thread by color and what is in my cupboard, not content like a purist.

3. Use the drawn sewing lines as a guide and free-motion straight stitch along all drawn lines. Sewing these stitches free-motion is much easier and faster than conventional straight-stitch sewing with a standard sewing foot. Be sure to stitch all drawn lines.

An alternate method is to satin stitch over all drawn lines. This uses much more thread and takes a lot more time. The resulting satin stitches, because they will be sewn twice, are much denser.

4. When cutting away the outside edges, you will need some stabilizer on the outside edge. To accomplish this, straight stitch through all layers about ½″ outside the outside edge of the motif. Call this the anchor line.

Once all the drawn lines are stitched, turn the work over and color in, on the bottom layer of the work, the background around your design, using the wash-out blue pen. This is especially helpful for beginners, as it makes cutting away the background foolproof. On the wrong side of the project cut away the background using sharp, pointed embroidery scissors. Cut away the stabilizer, if applicable, and the fabric, but leave the Solvy intact—do not cut through it. It will act as the stabilizer for the final satin stitching.

5. Cut away the background between the outside edge and the anchor stitch line without cutting the solvy. The fabric beyond the anchor stitch line will fall away after the project is completed. For now, it and the Solvy act as a temporary stabilizer.

6. Now set the machine to a narrow satin stitch, put on an appliqué foot, and reactivate the feed dogs. Lower the tension slightly. Set your machine to a short stitch length. Draw up the bobbin thread. There is no need to lockstitch to begin, but do lockstitch when you have finished stitching around the pattern. For details on satin stitching outside and inside points and curves, see Chapter 8, Appliquéd Leaf Jacket.

Adding Optional Cutwork Motifs

1. Outline details, such as veins in leaves, with a very narrow satin stitch.

2. Make flowers three-dimensional by layering three-dimensional appliqué motifs (see the next chapter).

3. Embellish cutwork with trims, ribbons, beads, and buttons. Refer to *Putting on the Glitz* for machine techniques.

"Aloha" Hat: Three-Dimensional Appliqué

Satin-Stitch Appliqué

Fabric motifs are used decoratively to enhance garments and quilts. The fabric motifs are backed with both cotton-blend batting and backing fabrics and satin stitched around the outside edges to seal in the batting and finish the raw edges of the fabrics. The bird on the hat of my "Aloha Diamond Head" garment is decorated with a three-dimensional appliqué motif.

MATERIALS

Scraps of cotton-blend batting
Fabric printed with distinctive
    motifs
Coordinated solid-color
    backing fabrics
Typing paper, wax paper,
    tearaway or water-soluble
    stabilizer
Thread to match background
Monofilament thread
Permanent felt marking pen
Open-toe appliqué foot
Straight pins
Sharp embroidery scissors

Creating the Appliqué

1. Cut out motifs from your fabric, leaving about 1" to 1½" beyond the printed outline.

2. Cut out a scrap of cotton-blend batting larger than the motif.

3. Cut out a scrap of coordinated fabric larger than the batting.

4. Layer motif, batting, and coordinated fabric (wrong sides toward batting). Use one or two straight pins to secure all three layers through the center.

5. Set your machine to a satin stitch (for details see Leaf Jacket). Satin stitch just outside the printed outline (the left swing of the needle will barely touch the outside of the motif).

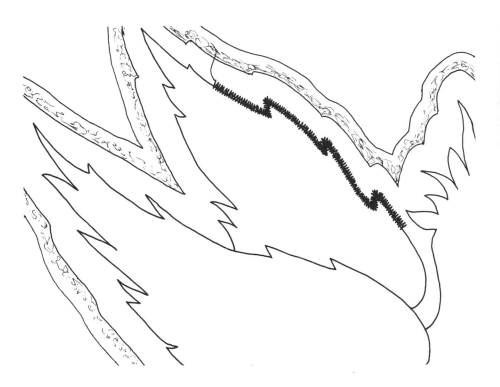

6. Cut off excess fabric and batting outside the satin-stitched edge.

110

7. Place the stabilizer (typing paper, freezer paper, tear-away, etc.) beneath the motif and return to the machine for a second round of satin stitching. If stabilizer is not used, the three-dimensional motif will ripple and probably will not lie flat.

ANN'S TIP. Use an open-toe appliqué foot for better visibility.

8. Remove the stabilizer after stitching.

9. Use the permanent felt marking pen to color any batting or stabilizer showing through the stitching.

Optional Machine Quilting

Machine quilting can add texture to and enhance the design of a motif. Free-motion machine quilting is easier, but you can use an even-feed foot (see Chapter 12, Traditional Hawaiian Appliqué by Machine).

ANN'S TIP. Quilt with metallic thread for more sparkle and interest.

Attaching the Motifs

Machine tack the motifs onto the background fabric, either singly or in multiple layers. Hold the garment or quilt up in the position it will be worn or shown. If any motifs flop or sag, add a tack so they hold their proper position.

Method 1. Thread your sewing machine with monofilament thread and bar tack the motifs in place, usually on two or more outside edges.

Method 2. If the motif is machine quilted, thread the machine with your quilting thread and straight stitch ½″ to 1″ over the outermost quilting at two opposite points. Resist the temptation to sew the motif all around its outer edge, because it will lie flat, losing its three-dimensional effect.

ANN'S TIP. Ultrasuede can be used alone for three-dimensional shapes, without batting or backing: just satin stitch around it.

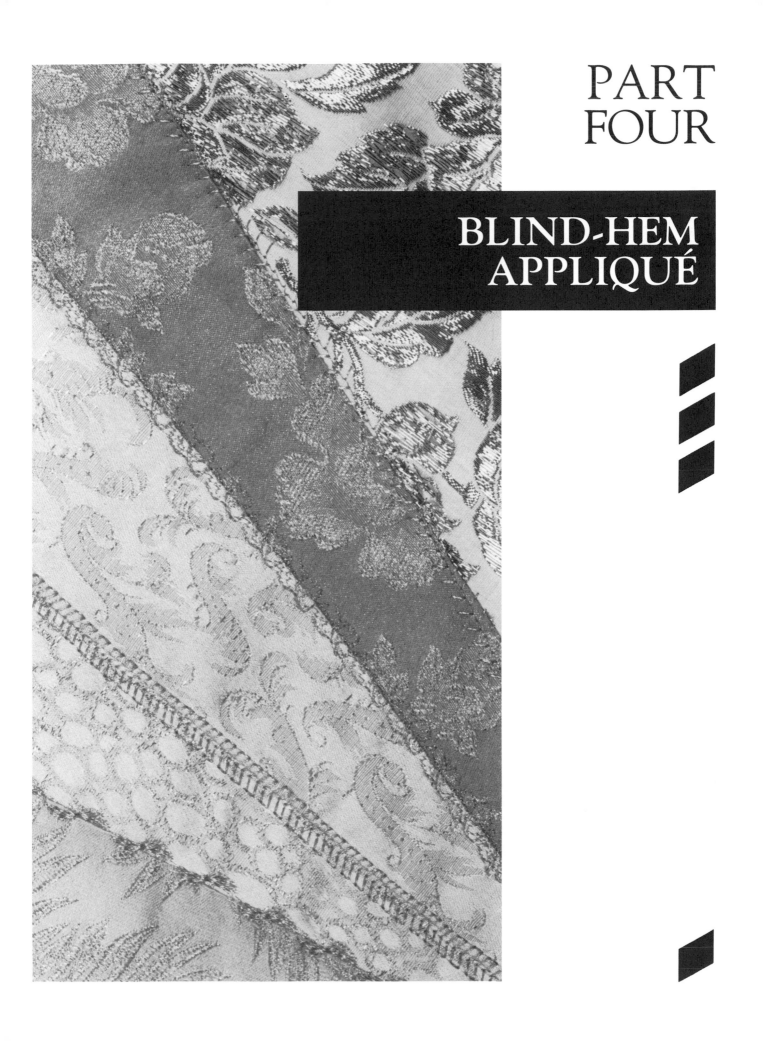

PART
FOUR

BLIND-HEM
APPLIQUÉ

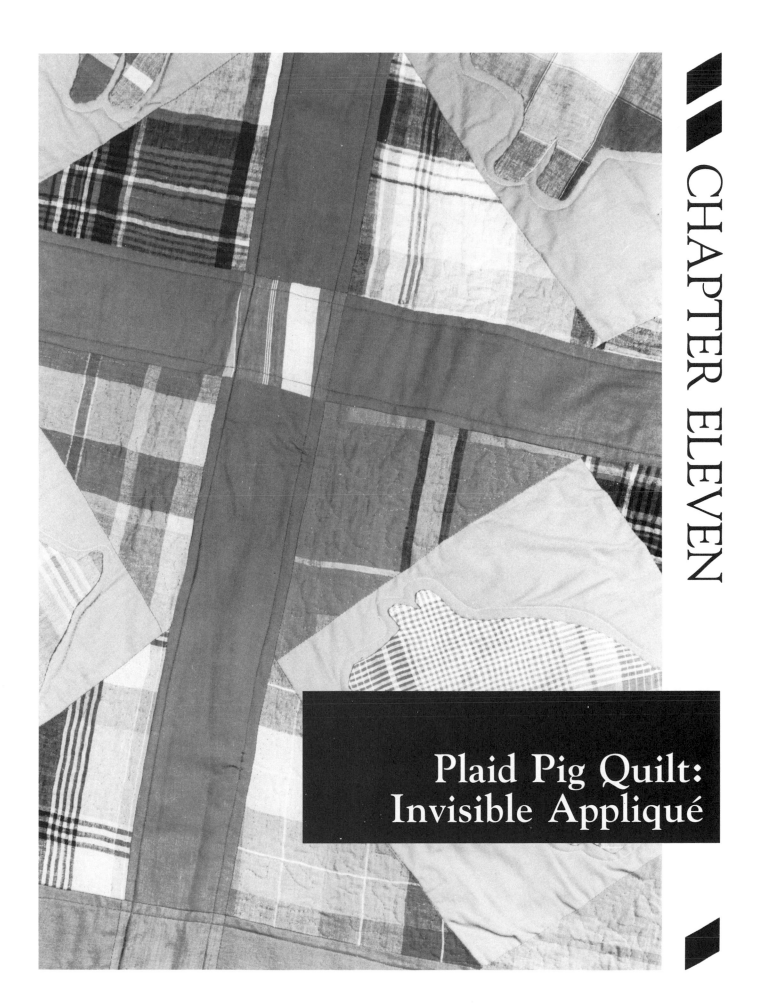

CHAPTER ELEVEN

Plaid Pig Quilt: Invisible Appliqué

We all hunt for fabric bargains. I was able to purchase a stack of Madras plaid salesman samples from an unusual store in New Hampshire, where the fabric is sold by the pound rather than measured by the yard. I thought it would be fun to make an animal quilt out of the plaids, as I am somewhat of a pig collector: I have a Calvin Swine watch; a strip-of-bacon watch; a "pigging out" necklace with pigs lying on cushions eating ice cream cones, chocolate chip cookies. It's obvious I *needed* a pig quilt to round out my collection!

The full-size quilt has twenty pig squares worked in invisible (blind-hem) appliqué. This method has several advantages:

- It resembles hand appliqué
- The thread doesn't cover up the multicolors of the fabrics
- It is quick and easy to do on almost all machines
- It requires no stabilizers

Preparing the Pigs for Appliqué

1. Transfer the full-size pig pattern at the end of this chapter to a piece of template material with a grease pencil. It's best to use clear plastic template material, like acetate, instead of cardboard because it will retain its edges. Cut out the template with a pair of scissors you use for paper.

2. Cut twenty pieces of different plaid fabrics of a size that will accommodate the pig template. Cut twenty pieces of a coordinating solid fabric of the same size as the plaids. Note: You may cut forty pieces of the plaids instead, if you prefer.

3. Lay down the twenty pieces of coordinating solid fabric, *or* twenty pieces of plaid if you are using all plaids, *right side up.*

4. Lay the twenty pieces of plaid for the pig appliqués *wrong side up* on top of the first twenty pieces.

5. Trace around the pig shape with a silver Berol pencil onto the *wrong* side of the twenty plaids, with the pig's snout and tail pointing to corners. The square is on point.

MATERIALS

⅓ yd. each of 20 different 44"–45" wide plaid prints

1½ yds. 44"–45" wide turquoise blue solid

2¼ yds. 44"–45" wide purple solid

5½ yds. 44"–45" wide blue solid for backing

Matching thread

Clear nylon monofilament thread

81" × 96" batting (full size)

Template material (acetate)

Grease pencil

Paper scissors

Silver Berol pencil

Chopstick

#1 noncorrosive safety pins

Evenfeed foot

Darning or spring foot

118

ANN'S TIP. Be sure all the pigs are drawn in the same direction (facing right or left, as you choose). An easy way to avoid confusion is to mark the top of the template with a piece of masking tape so you can keep the direction correct.

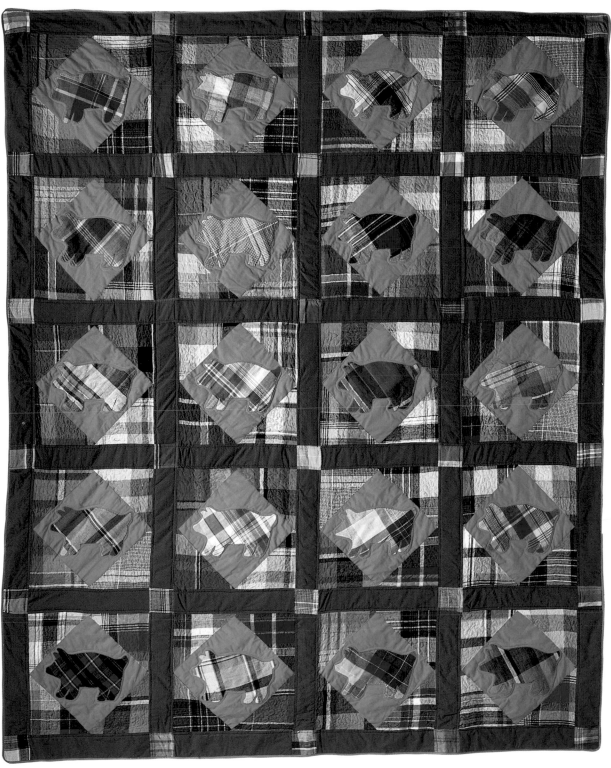

Plaid Pig Quilt, by author. Invisible appliqué (Ch. 11); machine quilted by Jeanne Elliott. *Photo courtesy of House of White Birches*

Broderie perse quilt, by author. Satin-stitch appliqué with invisible thread (Ch. 13); created for Fairfield Processing using Fabric Traditions cloth; machine quilted by Jeanne Elliott. *Photo by Mark Jenkins*

Butterfly quilt, by author. Blanket-stitch appliqué with VIP Fabrics; created for House of White Birches. *Photo by Mark Jenkins*

Hawaiian appliqué quilt, by author.
Needle-turn invisible appliqué (Ch. 12).
Photo courtesy of Pfaff Club magazine

6. Pin the paired fabrics together (pig drawing on top, solid or plaid backing beneath, with *right sides together*).

7. Straight stitch on the drawn line of each pig. Leave the needle in the fabric whenever you need to lift the presser foot to turn curves and points. You can use an open toe (appliqué) foot for this operation for greater visibility, but there is a slight tunnel under this foot; you will get a smoother seam with a standard foot. Plastic feet give better visibility. You might want to saw out the center of a clear appliqué foot to make it an open-toe foot.

ANN'S TIP. A Bernina presser foot knee lift frees the hands for easier turning.

ANN'S TIP. The standard snap-on foot (1A) on a Pfaff can be turned around and used as an open-toe foot.

---

8. Cut out the pig shapes ⅛″ outside the sewing line. Clip the inside corners and points to the stitches and clip off the outside corners.

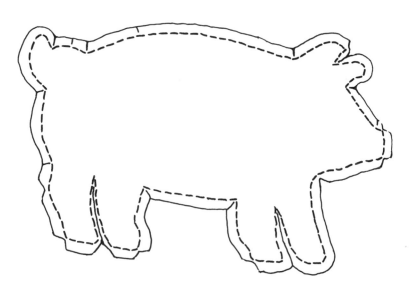

9. Making sure that all pigs are facing the desired direction, slit the center of the back side and turn the pigs through to the right side. Use a chopstick as a point turner; do not use scissor points or a skewer, because they will rip the fabric. Massage the fabric between your thumb and forefinger to smooth out curves. Press.

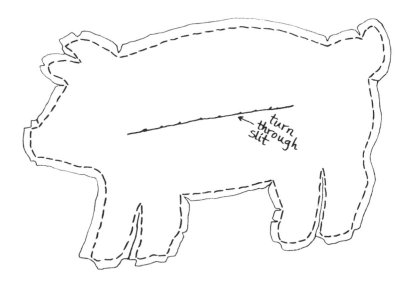

turn through slit

Setting Up Your Machine

1. Cut twenty 11½″ squares of turquoise fabric.

2. Pin a pig right side up in the center of each of the turquoise squares.

3. Thread the machine with clear monofilament.

4. Lower the tension slightly.

5. Thread the bobbin with a neutral thread. Some people like to use monofilament in the bobbin. If you want to use it, fill a metal bobbin; if you have no metal bobbins, fill a plastic one only half full, since monofilament may break the bobbin.

ANN'S TIP. On a Bernina, thread *regular* thread through the finger on the bobbin case.

6. Set the machine to a blind-hem stitch. On most machines the indicator for the setting looks like the picture below. This setting allows the appliqué to be sewn clockwise.

Some machines, on the other hand, have a setting that looks like this, a mirror image. This setting allows the appliqué to be sewn counterclockwise.

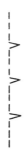

Some machines, particularly older Elnas, have small zigzag stitches instead of straight stitches between the bite stitches.

121

7. Use an appliqué foot on all machines; or use an open-toe appliqué foot. A utility straight-stitch foot can be used, but it has poor visibility for appliqué stitching.

If the machine is a Bernina computer machine and the screen says use a #5 foot, use the appliqué foot instead. The #5 foot is for blind-hem stitches, the original use, but not helpful in this application.

8. Set the stitch length on a computer machine at approximately 1.5. (A computer Elna machine is 1.8. This is all right.)

Some computer machines have preset settings; some will not go lower than 2.0. Sometimes pushing a mirror or turnover stitch button will lower the setting. If 2.0 is the lowest setting, it is all right.

On a computer Pfaff, increase the stitch length to 3.5. Push the twin needle button and the display will register a setting 3.5 mm lower, but will sew correctly at 1.5 mm.

On mechanical Berninas, tighten the stitch knob so that the line on the knob is at 12 o'clock. Loosen the knob 13 hours, to 11:00.

On conventional mechanical machines set the stitch length at a slightly loose machine appliqué setting, about 1½, or in the buttonhole setting.

9. Set the needle in the right-hand position for clockwise stitching. Set the needle in the left-hand position for counterclockwise stitching. Most computer machines require no change of needle position; everything is preprogrammed in the machine.

10. Set mechanical machines at a fairly narrow stitch width—between 1 and 2; preferably 1.5. Some mechanical or computer machines have a preprogrammed width. This will be acceptable only if the setting is wider than 1.5.

11. Test a few stitches to check balance. If the bobbin thread shows on the front, you can use monofilament in the bobbin. If finer monofilament thread is breaking in the machine, use a larger size.

ANN'S TIP. If the bobbin thread is showing on the front of the pigs, tighten the screw on the bobbin case, if possible. Remember to return the screw to its normal position after appliquéing.

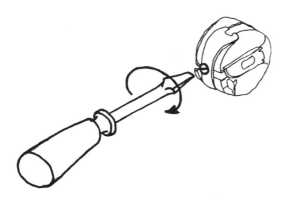

Blind-Hem Appliqué

1. The straight stitches always lie on the background fabric, and the "V" or bite stitches reach over onto the actual appliqué.

Backstitch the beginning stitches to secure the thread. Newer computer Elna machines will not backstitch except on straight stitches, so lock the stitches either by pushing the lockstitch button or by holding the fabric back and sewing in one place.

Some other newer computer machines have a lockstitch button which activates stitching just by pushing it; or you can reverse the blind-hem stitch to lock the stitches.

2. To sew an outside point, sew up *to* the outside point. Count the number of straight stitches between the pick stitches, usually three or five. If the bite stitch is not the stitch at the outside point, engage the reverse mechanism on the machine. Hold the fabric so it doesn't move. Continue sewing the straight stitches (count them!) until the bite stitch occurs.

ANN'S TIP. On a computer Elna, hold the fabric and sew in place. When the pick is sewn, raise the presser foot, turn the fabric, and continue to appliqué.

---

3. End the appliqué stitches by engaging the reverse stitch and sewing a few stitches to lock. Since you are sewing with monofilament thread, the reverse stitches will not show. If your computer machine has a lockstitch button, use it.

4. Press the appliquéd pigs on the wrong side of the fabric with the iron on a low setting. Too much heat may melt the monofilament thread.

Creating Patchwork

1. Cut forty 8½″ squares of the plaid fabrics. Cut these squares in half diagonally to form eighty plaid triangles. Use a rotary cutter, mat, and a plastic template for greater ease and accuracy.

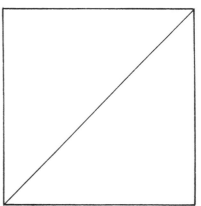

2. All patchwork is sewn with a ¼″ seam allowance. Use masking tape on the machine's throat plate (parallel to the foot) to mark a perfect ¼″ seam gauge.

ANN'S TIP. On a Bernina, move the needle position to the right one notch when using the utility sewing foot.

ANN'S TIP. On a computer Pfaff, move the needle position to 3> when using the utility sewing foot.

---

3. Sew a plaid triangle to each of the four sides of the squares with the pig appliqués. Use a different plaid for each side. Sew the triangles with the *wrong side* of the appliqué square on *top* of the triangles. This will prevent stretching of the bias edge of the triangle.

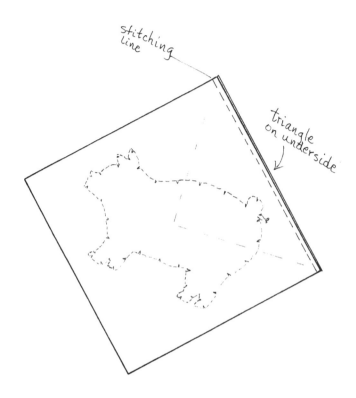

4. On a low setting, press and then trim these pieces to perfect 14½″ squares.

5. Cut forty-nine solid purple rectangles 3½″ × 14½″. Cut thirty 3½″ squares of plaid.

6. Sew a purple rectangle to the left side of a pig square; then another rectangle to the right side. Sew a second square to this rectangle. Continue until you have a row of five rectangles alternating with four squares, as shown. (Make four more rows following this same procedure.)

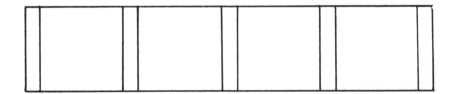

7. Sew six rows of sashing alternating the remaining rectangles and the 3½″ squares, following the sequence shown.

8. Assemble and sew the sashing rows, alternating with the rows of squares to form a quilt top.

Making the Quilt Sandwich

1. Cut the blue backing fabric into two pieces of equal length, 2¾″ yards.

2. Right sides together, sew these two halves parallel to the selvage to form the backing. Press the seam allowance to one side, not open.

3. Lay out the backing, *wrong side up*. Lay the batting on the backing, then lay the quilt top *right side up* on top of the batting.

ANN'S TIP. Unfold the batting and let it "breathe" for a couple of hours to smooth out wrinkles.

---

4. Pin-baste the quilt "sandwich" together with #1 (1″) non-corrosive safety pins. Pin about every 6″.

Machine Quilting the Quilt

1. Put an even-feed foot on the sewing machine and set the machine to a longer straight-stitch length, about 3.5–4.0, or 8–10 stitches per inch.

2. Stitch parallel to, and ¼″ from, all seam lines all over the quilt.

3. Outline quilt the twenty pigs. The easiest method is *free motion* or *outline* quilting. Set up your sewing machine for this method with a darning or spring foot; lower or cover the feed dogs. Set the stitch length to zero and thread the machine in a matching thread.

Lower the presser-bar lever. Draw up the bobbin thread to start. Sew several stitches in place to lock.

Remember that the feed dogs are immobile: You use your hands to move the fabric under the needle.

Slowly stitch around the pig silhouette on the background fabric. Lock the final stitches by sewing in place 5–6 stitches. Clip the threads.

ANN'S TIP. You may find it helpful to think that free-motion quilting is similar to the way you move your hands and arms to operate a Ouija board.

If you are not comfortable with free-motion quilting, you can straight stitch around the pigs by slowly stitching, lifting the presser foot, turning the fabric slightly, lowering the presser foot, and stitching. You will need to turn the entire quilt many times through the arm of the machine.

4. Quilt the plaid triangles with free-motion meander quilting. The stitching pattern looks like jigsaw puzzle pieces.

Ann's Quick Binding Method

1. Cut off the batting excess (*not* the backing!) ½" larger than the quilt top, all around the quilt.

2. Cut off the backing excess ½" larger than the batting (1" larger than the quilt top) all around the quilt.

3. Fold the backing forward onto the batting ½". Fold this strip of backing and batting again ½" onto the quilt top, pinning as you go. I use clover head pins for this step.

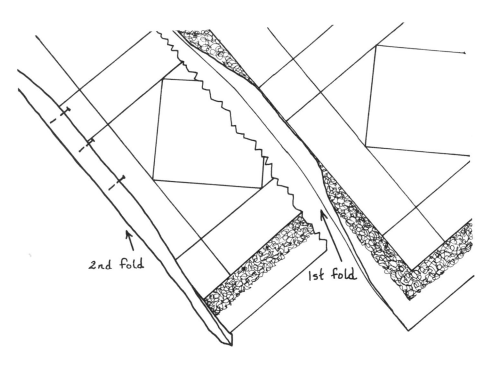

4. To miter the corners, cut off the batting diagonally across the corner ½" out from the quilt top's corner *before* folding over the edges as described in step 3.

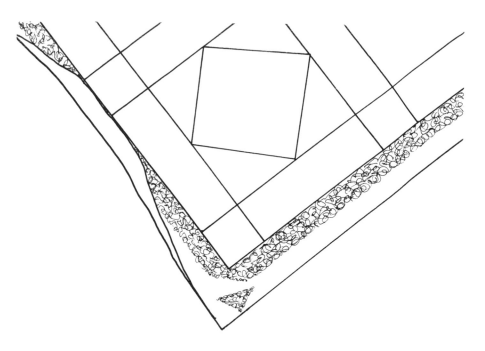

5. Cut off the backing diagonally across the corner ¼" outside and parallel to this cut batting edge.

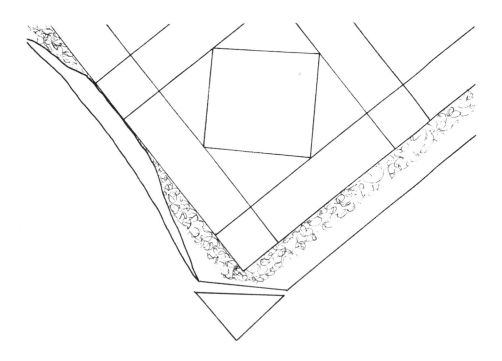

6. Fold the outside cut corner of the backing over about ¾″ and onto the quilt top.

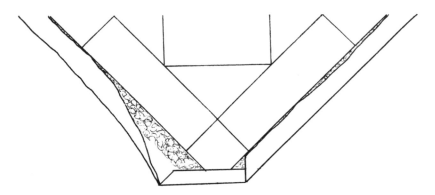

7. Fold the outside edges about ¾″ over the batting and then onto the quilt top to form mitered corners. Pin the folds as you go (see step 3).

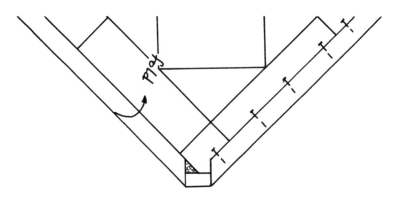

8. Set up your sewing machine for blind-hem stitching (the same setting used to appliqué the pigs). Thread the machine with monofilament thread.

9. Mirror (or "turn over") the blind-hem stitches, if possible. The stitch should look like this:

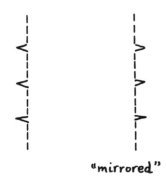

"mirrored"

Using the mirrored stitches will allow the quilt to lie outside the machine on the left side. If your machine will not mirror, roll the quilt tightly and maneuver it under the arm of the machine.

Stitch the binding in place, using the blind-hem stitch. The straight stitches fall on the quilt; the zigzag pick on the binding.

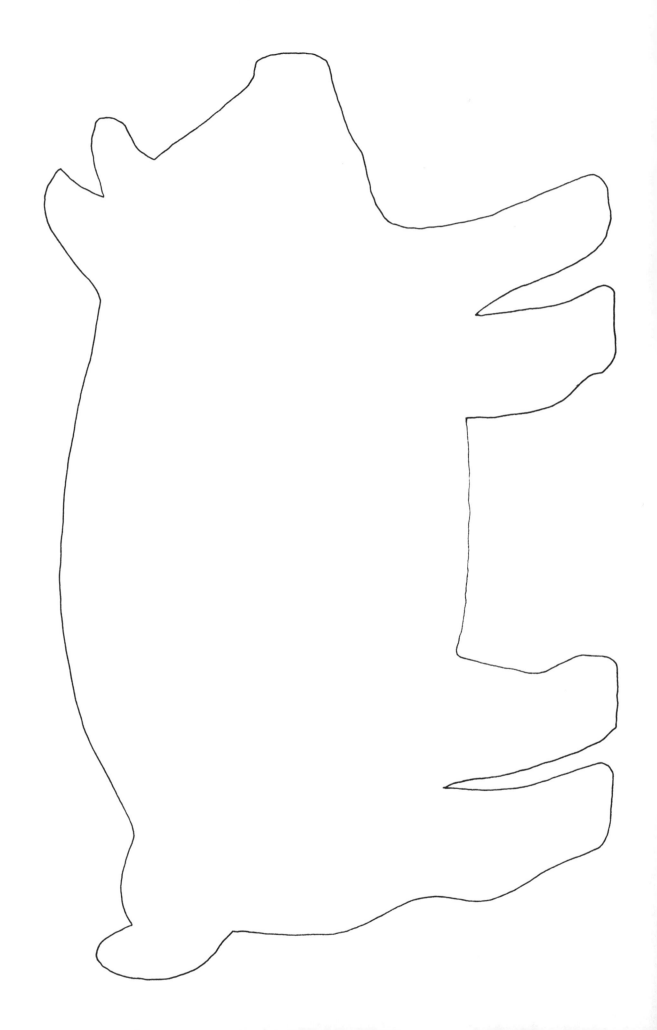

CHAPTER TWELVE

**Traditional Hawaiian
Appliqué by Machine**

I have been teaching sewing and quilting workshops in Honolulu, Hawaii, for several years. I have always had an interest in Hawaiian quilts; in fact, they are probably my favorite quilts.

Hawaiian quilting began in 1820 when missionaries traveled by ship to the Hawaiian Islands and tried to teach the native women traditional American quiltmaking. Prior to this time, Hawaiians made *tapas,* a bark cloth used for clothing and bedding. These tapa designs evolved into the traditional designs that are seen in Hawaiian quilts.

The Hawaiian appliqué design is made by folding a piece of fabric into eighths. The design is then traced onto the folded fabric and all eight layers are cut out at once. It's like making a paper snowflake. The first fold produces two layers; the second, four layers; third fold, eight layers.

MATERIALS

Monofilament thread

Neutral color thread for bobbin

Noncorrosive #1 safety pins

Sharp, pointed embroidery scissors

Hawaiian design quilt top in 100% cotton, fully basted

Thread to match the appliqués and background

Circular or darning foot

Walking or even feed foot

Bias binding to match the appliqués (optional)

Batting

Coordinated calico for backing

One Clover-pin or other long, plastic-head pin

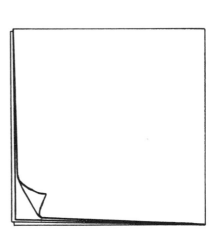

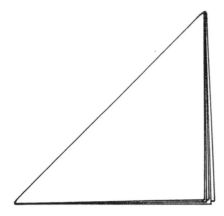

This cutout is then unfolded and basted onto a background fabric. Traditional Hawaiian quilts are made in strong colors: red, yellow, blue, green, and white. On Hawaiian quilts, the motifs are hand-appliquéd onto the background and echo quilted, usually ½″ in between the lines. The quilting lines radiate both outward from the appliqué and inward onto it. The minimum time required for a bed-size Hawaiian quilt, both appliqué and quilting, is six to nine months—nonstop. It is not unusual for the casual quilter to work for three years on a single quilt. For this reason, many quiltmakers shy away from this special type of quilt.

I was teaching a workshop in Iowa where one of my victims— I call all my students victims—told me of a quilt top she had bought several years earlier. She had realized that she would never finish it, having hand appliquéd only 12″ of a beautiful red design basted onto a navy ground. She sold it to me for $90, her original cost. I bought it as a challenge to modernize and make more accessible this wonderful technique.

ANN'S TIP. Use 100% cotton fabric as poly-cotton blends do not needle-turn easily, and they slip as you try to stitch them.

Since the appliqué design was already basted to the ground and was already clipped for turning at curves and corners, the obvious next step was to figure a way to turn the edges. I couldn't use any of the traditional methods I knew—freezer paper, gluestick, spray adhesive, sewing a second layer of fabric onto the edges—but the "Machine Queen" does no hand basting!

There are several methods of turning under edges that I do *not* personally use. One is to cut the actual appliqué shape out of Reynolds freezer paper and press it onto the wrong side of the fabric. Then cut the fabric ¼″ larger all around than the freezer paper.

Clip the edges to the paper.

Turn under and iron the raw edges onto the freezer paper.

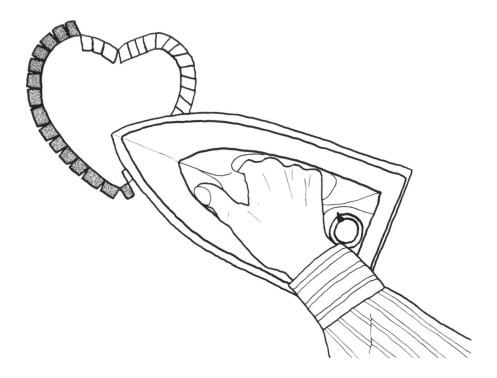

Pop the paper off and appliqué the shape in place. I personally do not do this because of the risk of burning my fingers.

The two "sticky" methods of appliqué, which I find tedious and messy, require cutting the appliqué shape from a piece of plastic or cardboard template material. Trace around the template onto fabric with a silver Berol pencil.

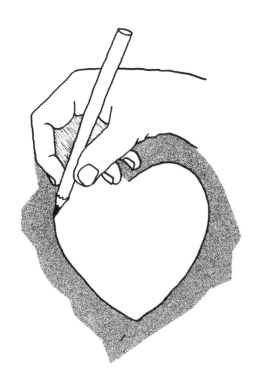

Cut the shape out of fabric ¼″ larger all around than the template.

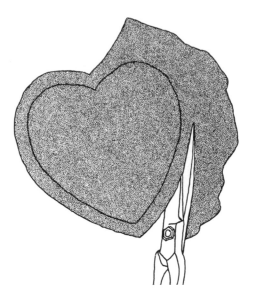

Then clip and turn the raw edges, pressing them toward the back, and use either a gluestick or a spray adhesive to place the appliqué on the background for stitching.

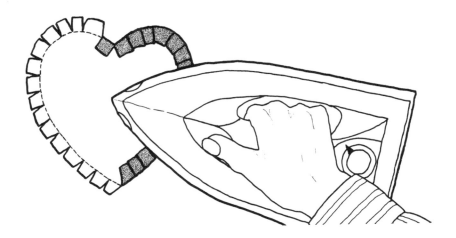

One of the traditional methods for hand appliqué is a needle-turn technique, accomplished by using the sharp point of a hand needle to turn under the raw edges of fabric about 1″–2″ in front of the hand stitching as you stitch. The turned edges are finger-pressed and held down with the other hand's fingers until the turned edge is appliquéd in place.

I decided to try this needle-turn technique by machine. First, I set the machine for a narrow blind-hem pattern and turned under the raw edges in front of the stitching.

Set your machine at a narrow blind-hem stitch, with the width between 1 and 2. Also set the stitch length between 1 and 2. Use an appliqué or open-toe foot. If necessary, position the needle in the right-hand position for clockwise stitching or in the left-hand position for counterclockwise (mirror image) stitching. On most computerized machines the needle position is preprogrammed.

For more details on setting up various machine models, see the section on blind-hem appliqué in Chapter 11, Plaid Pig Quilt.

Thread the machine with monofilament thread and a neutral regular thread in the bobbin. If the bobbin thread shows on the front, use monofilament in the bobbin. See tips on the use of monofilament thread in Chapter 3.

Ann's Appliqué Method

Begin stitching on the outside edge of the appliqué. (Note that traditional hand appliqué is started in the center motif, but because the basted quilt top will be turned through the center of the machine, there will be too much fraying of raw edges if the appliqué is done from the center outward.)

ANN'S TIP. Do not use any tear-off stabilizer. It is cumbersome, and there won't be much distortion of the fabric anyway.

The straight stitches are to lie on the background fabric, and the "V" or bite stitches reach over onto the actual appliqué. Backstitch the beginning and ending stitches to secure the thread, or use a lockstitch button if your machine has one.

Begin stitching on a long curved edge, not at an outside or inside point. Use the Clover pin to turn under the raw edges in front of the sewing foot. Slide the pin point under raw edges toward you, turning under a little fabric as you go. Turn under only ⅛″, not ¼″. The straight stitches fall on the background and the bite stitches reach over onto the appliqué.

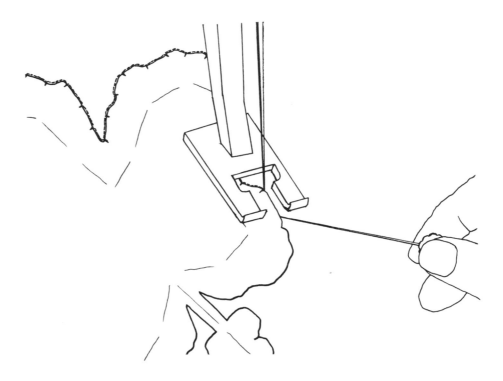

For inside points:

1. Sew up to the inside point, leaving the needle in the appliqué fabric.

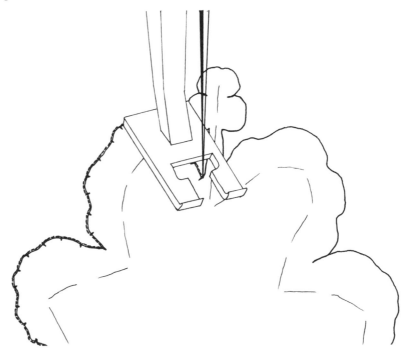

2. Lift the presser foot and turn the fabric around, preparing to stitch in the opposite direction with the needle still in the fabric.

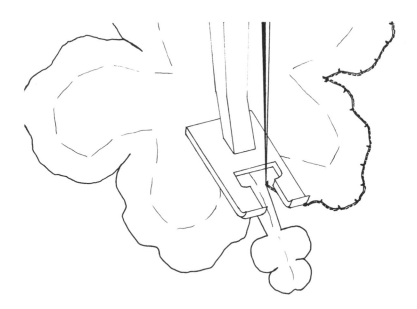

3. With the Clover pin turn under the fabric to be stitched; finger press.

4. Use the Clover pin to push a slight tuck of puckered, turned-under fabric against the sewing machine needle.

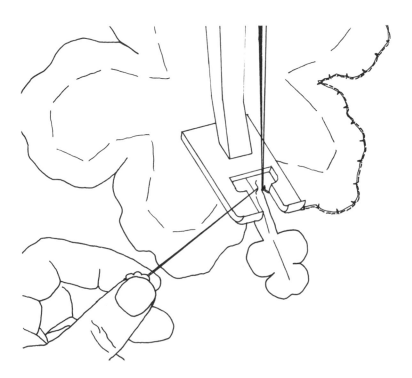

5. Holding the tuck with the pin, begin stitching and catch the tuck in it. Remove the pin. The tuck will flatten if you run your fingernail across it.

Continue your appliquéing.

For outside points:

1. Pin-turn the raw edge all the way off the point. Stop stitching about ⅜″ from the point's end, leaving the needle down in the background fabric.

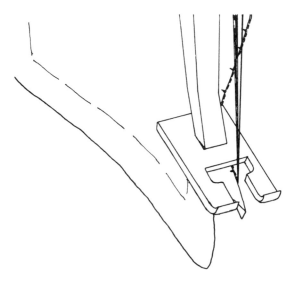

2. Clip off the "dog ear" (the turned-under bit of raw edge that sticks out beyond the edge of the unappliquéd side of the point) flush with the point's raw edge. With the needle still in the fabric, lift the presser foot for easier access to clip off this point.

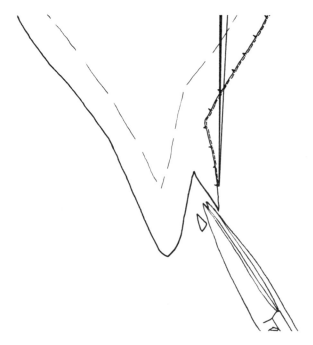

3. Turn the fabric around. With the pin point turn under the excess fabric into the point. The stitches on the left side provide a "pusher" against which to work.

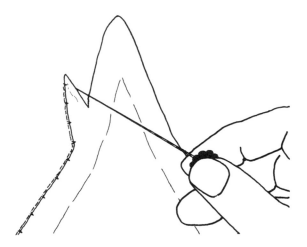

4. Adjust the needle so it goes back into the same pivot hole. Stitch two or three straight stitches just at the point to anchor the turned fabric, and then return to blind-hem stitch.

5. Continue appliquéing the entire outside edge.

143

6. Appliqué the next inside edge; work toward the center of the quilt until all appliquéing is complete. Appliqué interior slashes last, if your design has them.

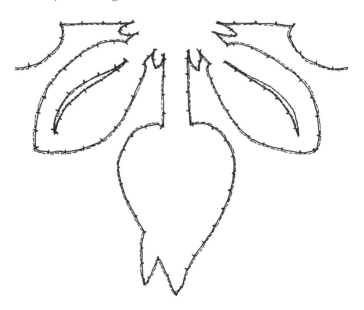

Hawaiian or Echo Quilting

1. Make up the backing a little bigger than the quilt top. If you seam two pieces of calico, press the center seam to one side. Lay out the backing, batting, and quilt top. Pin baste all layers of the quilt together every six inches or less, using #1(1″) noncorrosive safety pins.

ANN'S TIP. Hawaiian quilters use 100% polyester batting because of the tropical climate. I prefer to work with cotton/ polyester batting.

---

2. Put a circular or darning foot on the sewing machine.

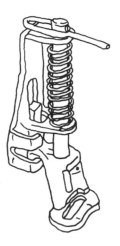

3. Lower or cover the feed dogs for free-motion quilting. If free-motion quilting is not comfortable for you, change the machine back to a longer straight stitch and use a walking or evenfeed foot. This will be tedious, however, even with a Bernina knee-lift lever, because you will constantly have to lift and lower the presser foot.

ANN'S TIP. Although traditional Hawaiian quilting was done with white thread, many native quiltmakers now use thread colors that match their two fabrics, for example, red on red, blue on blue.
Contemporary Hawaiian quilters sometimes use a coordinating calico backing instead of the classic solid, eliminating the need for an exact bobbin thread color match.

---

4. Thread the machine to match the background fabric color.

5. On the background, outline the quilt center appliqué motif first with free-motion quilting. Outline the cutout center, if your design has one.

6. Change the thread color back to the appliqué color and quilt an "echo" line *parallel to*, and *inside*, the edge of the appliqué, about ½" to ⅝" inside it.

7. Continue each parallel echo line inward until the quilt center appliqué motif is quilted. The quilting should look like water rippling after a stone is thrown into it (see step 9).

8. If there is an outside appliqué border, change the thread back to the background color and outline quilt inside the inner appliqué border motif.

9. Echo quilt radiating parallel lines outward from the quilt center appliqué motif and inward from the border motif.

10. Continue quilting background back and forth inward from each appliqué motif until background is quilted. The two innermost quilting lines will be in the center of the background.

11. Change the thread color back to the appliqué color and repeat steps 6 and 7 until the outer appliqué motif is quilted.

12. If there is more background on the outside edge, change the thread back to the background color and outline the outer appliqué around the motif.

13. Continue echo quilting the background until the quilting is completed.

Curved-Corner Binding

A lot of traditional Hawaiian quilts have curved corners. Here is my technique for making them:

1. Trim the excess batting and backing flush with the quilt top.

2. To curve the edges, fold one corner in half diagonally.

3. Cut off a curved edge.

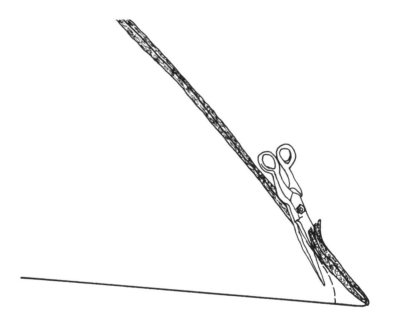

4. Unfold the corner to check the accuracy and symmetry of the cut. Use this rounded corner as a pattern to shape the other three corners.

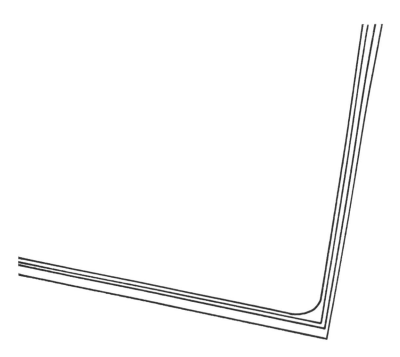

5. Sew bias binding (to match the color of your appliqué) around all the outside edges of the quilt top, with the right sides of the binding and quilt top together.

6. Fold the remaining binding onto back edge of quilt and hand stitch it in place.

ANN'S TIP. Sorry! There's no really good sewing machine remedy for this hand stitching. One possibility is to sew the binding onto the back and machine blind-hem the front edge with monofilament thread—but machine-stitched bindings will not win ribbons in quilt shows.

CHAPTER THIRTEEN

Broderie Perse
Appliqué

Chintz fabrics were first manufactured in the 1800s. Quilters liked to cut out the motifs and hand appliqué them onto a solid color background. There are several methods to machine appliqué these motifs.

Method 1: Outer-Edge Satin Stitch

Fabrics appropriate for this type of appliqué have motifs printed with space around them. They may be floral, animal and bird, or novelty prints. Your background fabric should be a solid of exactly the same color as the background of the print fabric, and your thread color should match.

1. Cut a square of paper-backed fusible web larger than the motif to be cut out.

2. Fuse the web onto the wrong side of the fabric, being sure that the motif is covered completely. Use a dry iron to fuse paper-backed fusible web. Press on the paper side with a dry, not steam, iron. If you need to add another piece of web, butt two straight edges—do not overlap.

3. Cut out around the fused motif about ⅛″ outside the printed outline. Don't use your best fabric scissors.

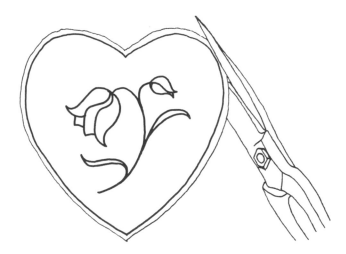

4. Peel the paper off of the back of the fabric. To start the peel, roll the edge of the paper and the paper and fabric will separate. If the pulled-off paper does not feel smooth and has bumps of webbing on it, repress the paper onto the fabric.

5. Position the motif on the background fabric and press to fuse it in place.

MATERIALS

Print fabrics with motifs appropriate for appliqués, such as chintz

Matching solid background fabric

Thread to match background

Nylon monofilament thread

Paper-backed fusible web (optional)

Tear-off stabilizer (optional)

6. Cut a square of tear-off stabilizer to pin behind the appliqué.

7. Thread the machine with a color that matches the background fabric.

ANN'S TIP. Use a rayon thread on a shiny chintz fabric.

Set the machine to a medium zigzag width and a short stitch length: 6 o'clock on a mechanical Bernina; below the #1 stitch length; or halfway in the buttonhole setting, depending on your machine.

Attach an appliqué foot to the machine. The groove underneath the foot allows the bulky satin stitch to move through the machine.

Lower the upper tension slightly. Draw up the bobbin thread. There is no need to lockstitch until you have stitched all the way around the appliqué. For details on satin stitching outside points, inside points, and curves, see Chapter 8, Appliquéd Leaf Jacket.

8. Satin stitch around the entire motif. The outer stitching should be off the edge of the appliqué; the inner edge of the stitching should barely touch the printed outline of the motif.

9. Tear off the stabilizer and press. Always press appliqués on the *wrong* side of the fabric.

Method 2: Blind-Hem Stitch

This appliqué method will look more like original hand appliqué. The motifs you use should be the same types as those for the previous method.

1. Cut out each motif roughly, leaving about 1″ of the print's background around each motif.

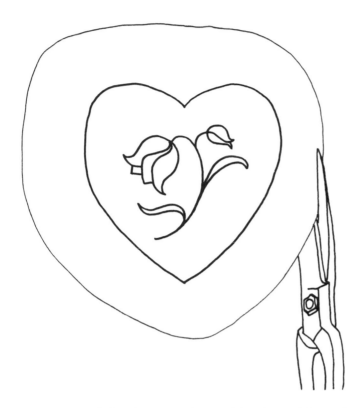

2. Cut out a solid-color coordinated backing fabric the same approximate size as the motif.

3. Pin the two layers together, right sides together, using one or two straight pins in the center.

4. Straight stitch around the entire edge of the motif—leave no opening.

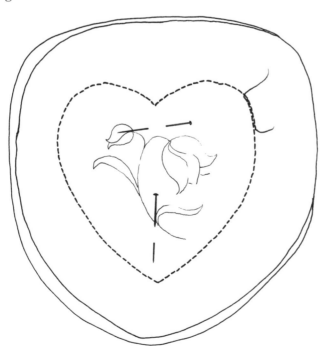

155

5. Trim off excess fabric to ⅛″ outside the stitching line. Clip inside points and clip off outside corners. Slit the center of the solid backing, taking care not to cut through the motif fabric.

6. Turn the motif through the slit to the right side.

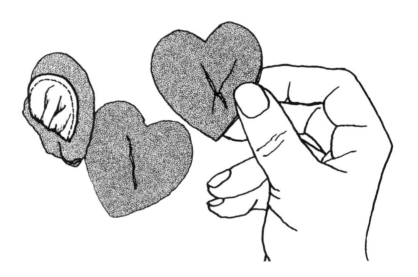

ANN'S TIP. If no point turner is available, use a chopstick. Do not use a sharp instrument; it may puncture the fabric.

7. Press the turned motif.

8. Blind-hem stitch the appliqué in place onto the background you've chosen.

Set your machine to a narrow blind-hem stitch, with the width between 1 and 2. Set the stitch length also between 1 and 2. Use an appliqué or open-toe appliqué foot. If necessary, position the needle in the right-hand position for clockwise stitching or in the left-hand position for counterclockwise (mirror image) stitching. On most computerized machines the needle position is preprogrammed.

Thread the machine with monofilament thread and a neutral regular thread in the bobbin. If the bobbin thread shows on the front, use monofilament thread in the bobbin. See tips on the use of monofilament in Chapter 3, Threads for Appliqué.

For more details on setting up various sewing machine models, see the section on blind-hem appliqué in Chapter 11, Plaid Pig Quilt.

The blind-hem straight stitches are to lie on the background fabric and the "V" or bite stitches reach over onto the actual appliqué. Backstitch or lockstitch the beginning and ending stitches to secure the thread.

When you come to an outside point, be sure that a bite stitch catches the point. To achieve that you may need to reverse a few straight stitches while holding the fabric in place until you get a bite stitch. Count the number of straight stitches between bite stitches, usually three or five, on your machine.

9. Press the finished appliqué on the wrong side on a low iron setting so the nylon thread won't melt.

Method 3: Monofilament Satin Stitch

With this appliqué method you can cut out motifs on their printed edge, because the monofilament thread allows the motif pattern to show through. You can eliminate the tedious turning and sewing necessary for the two previous methods.

Follow steps 1 through 6 of Method 1: Outer-Edge Satin Stitch appliqué, at the beginning of this chapter.

1. Thread the upper sewing machine with monofilament thread. See tips for using monofilament in Chapter 3, Threads for Appliqué.

157

ANN'S TIP. Use clear monofilament thread with light fabrics, smoke-colored with darker fabrics.

---

2. Thread the bobbin with a matching regular thread. Test stitch: You want no show-through of the bobbin thread—or, at most, a bare minimum. If you get show-through, use monofilament in the bobbin.

3. Set the machine to a narrow zigzag width, between #1 and #2 or "narrow."

4. Set the stitch to a slightly loose zigzag: Too tight a stitch will cause lumps and interfere with even stitching.

5. Satin stitch around the entire motif. Refer to Method 1 for details on satin stitch.

Other Methods

See Chapter 12, Traditional Hawaiian Appliqué by Machine, for alternative edge-turning methods. In addition, there is a method of turning edges by using fusible interfacing as the lining fabric. This method is a little tricky: Sew the fusible interfacing onto the appliqué shape with the glue side facing the right side of the fabric. Slit the interfacing and turn the appliqué to the right side. Your appliqué will have finished edges and a backing that can be fused into place. The disadvantages to this method are that (1) the interfacing is white, grey or black, so unless it matches your project, it needs to be tucked carefully under all edges; and (2) the appliqué cannot be prepressed to smooth out the edges.

Another method is to use water-soluble Solvy film, sewn as above. The Solvy dissolves with water, leaving only your single layer of appliqué. Some fabrics, such as satin, cannot be put in water, so this method is limited to washable fabrics.

Appliqué shapes can also be prepared with a straight-stitch method:

1. Straight stitch around your drawn shape on the drawn line.

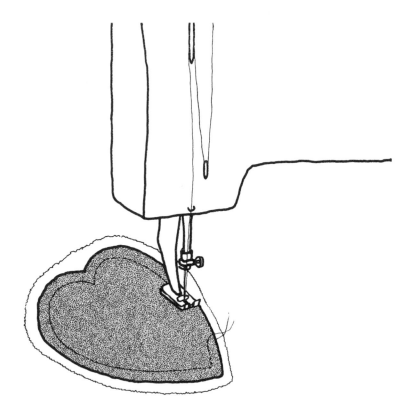

2. Clip up to the stitching line.

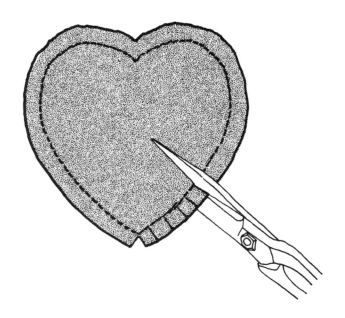

3. Turn under the clipped edges just inside the stitching line. As an alternative to pressing, turn the edge and machine baste.

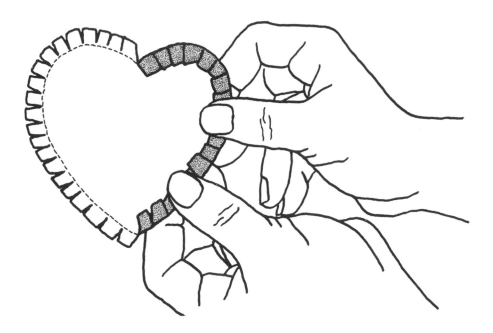

DECORATIVE
STITCH APPLIQUÉ

Toby's Collar:
Shadow Appliqué

At a class I taught for the Long Island Quilters Guild, one of my victims, Toby Davidson, wore an eye-catching collar (see color section). She sells her designs by mail (see Toby O. Creations, Sources of Supply.) On closer inspection, I discovered that this collar was actually an innovative form of shadow appliqué.

The traditional shadow appliqué technique is to cut out appliqué shapes and fuse them to a background fabric, and then to overlay sheer fabric, such as organdy, creating the softened colors and the "shadow" effect that gives the name. The sheer fabric is joined to the background by straight stitching around all the edges of the appliqué shapes. You will frequently see this technique on French hand-sewn garments, especially on collars of blouses and dresses.

The method that Toby used, the one described here, is a little more creative for sewing-machine work. It looks both traditional and contemporary. She used as background fabric a white polka dot on black. She fused flowers and leaves in traditional pastel colors, overlaid organdy and then did her machine work. Embellish the collar pieces, cut 1″ bigger all around than the pattern pieces, before construction.

MATERIALS

Collar pattern
White polka dot on black
  background fabric
Pastel fabrics for appliqués
Organdy for overlay
Gold metallic thread
Black thread
Darning, embroidery, or spring
  foot
Tailor-tack foot
Paper-backed fusible web
Black bias tape
Black buttons

How to Shadow Appliqué

1. Toby chose Talon gold metallic thread (see tips for using metallic thread in Chapter 3). She set up her sewing machine for free-motion work. Lower the feed dogs or cover them with a separate plate. Use a darning foot, embroidery foot, or spring foot.

On some machines, particularly Vikings, the presser-foot dial should be set on "darning", a "#" at the bottom of the numbers. On newer Pfaffs there are three levels on the presser-foot handle. Use the middle level for free-motion sewing.

Before you sew, you must lower the presser-foot lever to engage the top tension. The fabric must be able to move freely between the sewing-machine foot and the feed dogs. If your machine doesn't have adequate room, remove the cover plate. You will still be able to sew free-motion with the feed dogs exposed. On most machines the stitch length should be set to 0 to minimize wear and tear on the feed dogs. They still move on higher stitch settings when they are dropped.

2. Instead of straight-stitch outlines of the appliqué shapes, she used free-motion squiggle stitches. These stitches are open, and not dense.

ANN'S TIP. If your machine has decorative stitches, you could use open decorative stitches and save yourself a lot of work.

---

3. Work around all appliqué edges. Use straight stitches for details such as veins on leaves.

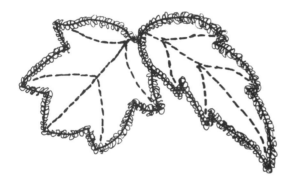

4. Decorate the centers of the flowers with metallic thread sewn with a tailor-tack foot.

The ridge in the center of the foot forms loops which fall off the back of the foot and look like unclipped turkey work. Sew a spiral to complete the center.

ANN'S TIP. Use a dab of Fraycheck on the underside of the loops to seal stitches.

---

5. Toby chose to fill in some of the background with random free-motion stitching with the gold thread. You may or may not choose to do this step.

6. To construct the collar, re-cut the pieces to the same size as the pattern pieces. To finish the collar, bind it with black bias tape and fasten it with black buttons and fabric loops.

CHAPTER FIFTEEN

Bomber Jacket:
Beyond Traditional
Machine Appliqué

Today's sewing machines have opened up a new territory for machine appliqué. I used decorative stitches for appliqué on a jacket for a fashion show. I had collected fabrics in both fire and ice colors for previous Fairfield Fashion Shows. One of my quilting friends, Rachel Kinsey Clark, of Watsonville, California, exclaimed, "I love that you do the elements in your Fairfield garments. I can't wait to see 'Earth'." I had not yet decided what to make for a garment in the 1991–92 Fairfield Fashion Show, but thanks to Rachel, I collected a bunch of "earth" fabrics: dark golds, rusts, greens. Herman Phynes III of Vogue/Butterick sent me a tracing—it had not yet been printed— of a bomber jacket pattern. I chose variegated and dark gold metallic threads from Sulky. With this arsenal I was ready to attack the bomber!

I decided to cut the top part of the jacket apart and appliqué triangles onto the background fabric. I added a band across the middle section and covered the bottom half of the jacket front, back, and sleeves with clamshell shapes. The upper sections of the jacket are appliquéd triangles of a brighter print.

Preparing Garment Sections

I cut out all the jacket sections in muslin 1″ larger than the pattern pieces. Stay stitch the fabric for the top section background (I used wavy cotton) onto the muslin for that section. The fabric for the triangles was a funky Alexander Henry print.

1. Fuse the wrong side of the print fabric for the triangles with paper-backed fusible web.

MATERIALS

Bomber jacket pattern

Various earth-tone and metallic fabrics

Variegated and dark gold metallic thread

Muslin

Lining

Paper-backed fusible web

Template material (acetate)

Grease pencil

Paper scissors

Silver Berol pencil

Batting or tear-off stabilizer

168

2. Make a triangle template from the pattern here.

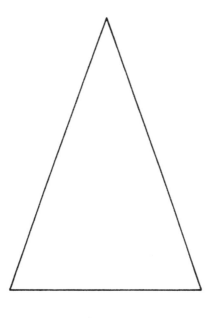

——————————————

ANN'S TIP. Clear plastic template material allows you to choose specific areas of print as you draw triangles.

——————————————

3. Trace around the triangle template on the paper side of the fabric and then cut out the triangles.

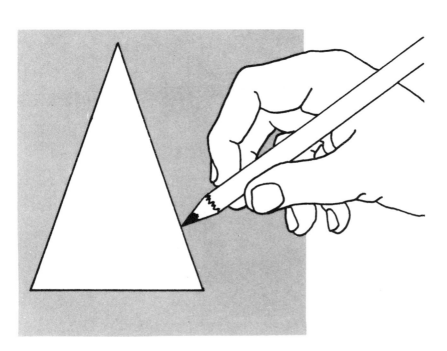

4. Remove the paper backing from the triangles. To make fast work of removing paper-backed fusible webbing, "slash" the back side of your work with a straight pin and tear the paper from the slit—much easier than starting at the outside edge.

5. Arrange and fuse the fabric triangles onto the top front and back sections of the jacket.

6. I chose to use batting beneath the garment sections as a stabilizer. If you prefer not to use batting, you can use tear-off stabilizer. Appliquéing through the batting substitutes for machine quilting.

Appliquéing Triangles

Some machines have a flame stitch built into them. The narrow part of the stitches is the same coverage as a narrow zigzag stitch. Every few stitches the needle swings so a "random" wider stitch occurs. This stitch can be used as a shading stitch when combined with other colors.

If you don't have a flame stitch, use a satin stitch for appliquéing. For details on satin-stitch appliqué refer to Chapter 8, Appliquéd Leaf Jacket.

ANN'S TIP. Use a variegated thread on a print background for an interesting effect.

To turn a corner:

1. Measure the widest width of the flame stitch and stop stitching that distance from the corner with the needle in the background fabric.

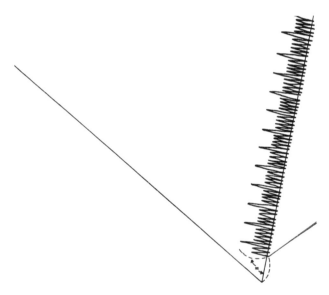

2. Raise the presser foot and turn the fabric clockwise. Reposition the needle (using the fly wheel) to the right hand swing so the stitch begins at the extreme top right of the corner. Stitch toward the next corner. After a few stitches, the fabric may have to be adjusted slightly if your corner is not a right angle.

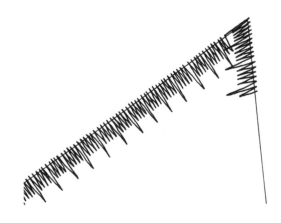

171

3. Repeat until all three corners are covered.

Using Decorative Stitching

The bottom of the jacket and sleeves are covered with clam-shells fused in place in rows overlapping each other. I used a variety of fabrics: silks, gold-printed cotton, acetates, satins, velvet, and lamés, to achieve a textured look. Mix up a range of colors for an interesting effect.

1. Make a template from the figure below. Again, clear plastic material lets you see the pattern of the fabric you are using and it will last a long time.

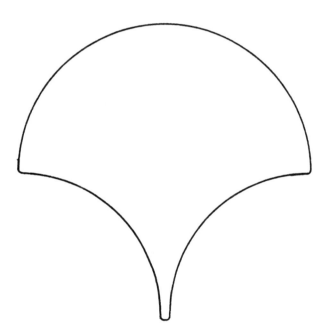

2. Fuse the wrong side of the fabrics for the clamshells with paper-backed fusible web. Then trace around clamshells on the paper side of the fabric and cut out. Remove the paper backing.

3. Begin at the top edge of the area to be covered and place one row of clamshells. Fuse in place.

4. Add the second row, being sure to slightly cover or butt against the first row of clamshells.

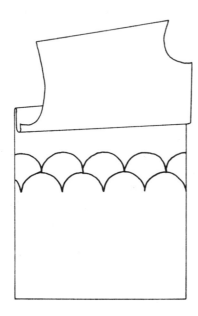

5. If you are unsure of color placement, pin all rows of clamshells in place before fusing. Cover the garment surface completely to the outside edges, row by row.

Dense Stitching. Be sure to use dense decorative stitch patterns to finish the edges of the appliquéd shells. The open, lacy ones will not cover raw edges of fabric. As with regular satin-stitch appliqué, always start with the bottom layer when there is an overlapped edge. End by appliquéing the top layers.

1. Start stitching at the left outside edge of each of the clamshells. Lockstitch the beginning of each decorative stitch.

ANN'S TIP. Mix up stitch patterns so that no two consecutive clamshells have the same design.

---

2. Decoratively stitch the entire curved edge; stop stitching at the end of the curve. The end of the curved edge may be a point in the middle of a decorative stitch. This is all right. See the next step.

3. Most computer sewing machines are preprogrammed to sew through the entire stitch pattern in a decorative stitch; so even if you push the lockstitch button to stop, the machine will complete the original stitch pattern before locking off. To get around this problem, change to another stitch pattern and then push the lockstitch button. On a newer Pfaff, push #19. Return the machine to straight stitch, lower stitch length to zero, and take 2 or 3 stitches.

4. Continue covering all raw edges until the clamshells are completed. The top row will be the last row.

ANN'S TIP. Clamshells could be added to the edges of your own garments and quilts. Clamshells also would be wonderful as fish scales on appliquéd fish.

Open Stitching. These stitches will not cover raw edges of fabric. They should be used decoratively only over sewn seams.

An example of using these stitches is the Oriental style jacket in Chapter 5, which has patchwork across the center in a fan design. All the patchwork seams are overworked with open decorative stitches in gold metallic thread.

There are a couple of rayon ribbon threads available, one from Elna, and the other from Rhode Island Textile Co. These are about ⅛" wide and can be sewn onto fabric with decorative stitches. (My jacket was sewn on an Elna 9000). Wind the ribbon thread onto the bobbin. Leave the end loose (do not put it through the conventional bobbin thread guide). When the bobbin is inserted into the case, guide the loose ribbon thread underneath the left-hand side of the bobbin holder with the help of a needle threader.

Increase the upper tension to #9 and set the machine to a decorative feather stitch pattern. Sew these stitches on the wrong side of the fabric. I sewed the vines for the leaves across the bottom edge of the jacket. I later satin stitched purple leaves onto the vines.

Finishing

Construct the jacket and lining according to the pattern directions.

Sources of Supplies

Following is a list of good mail-order sources for equipment, materials, embellishments, and supplies. Regardless of where you live, your choices should not be limited to what is available in your area. Just sit down with a pen and paper (or telephone) and contact the company or business you want from this list. Many of them have free catalogs or helpful brochures to help you make your decisions.

BATTING

Cedarburg Wollen Mill, W62 N 580 Washington Ave., Cedarburg, WI 53012. 1-800-W15-WOOL. *Wool batting; down/feather.*

Fairfield Processing, P.O. Box 1130, Danbury, CT 06813. *Polyester and blend battings and stuffings.*

Heartfelt, Box 1829, Vineyard Haven, MA 02568. *100% wool batting.*

Hobbs Bonded Fibers, 345 Owen Lane, Suite 114, Waco, TX 76710. *Send SASE for information about their polyester batting.*

Stearns Technical Textiles Company, Mountain Mist Consumer Products, 100 Williams St., Cincinnati, OH 45215-6316. (800) 345-7150. *Manufacturers of both polyester and 100% cotton battings.*

Taos Mountain Wool Works, P.O. Box 327, Arroyo Hondo, NM 87513. (505) 776-2925. *Wool battings.*

Warm Products, Inc., 11232 120th NE #112, Kirkland, WA 98033. (800) 234-WARM. *Manufacturers of Warm & Natural batting.*

YLI Corp., 482 N Freedom Blvd., Provo, UT 84601. (800) 854-1932. *Suppliers of silk batting, novelty threads for sewing, serging, and embroidery. Catalog $1.50.*

SEWING MACHINES

Bernina of America, Inc., 3500 Thayer Ct., Aurora, IL 60504-6182. (708) 978-2500. *Sewing machines, sergers, Create-A-Space Table.*

Elna, Inc., 7642 Washington Ave. S., Minneapolis, MN 55344. *Sewing machines, sergers, pressing machines.*

Fox Sewing Machines, Inc., 307 W. 38th St., New York, NY 10018. *Sells and repairs industrial sewing equipment. Sells steam irons and cutting machines.*

New Home Sewing Co., 100 Hollister Rd., Teterboro, NJ 07608. (201) 440-8080. *Sewing machines, Janome silk threads.*

Pfaff American Sales Corp., 610 Winters Ave., Paramus, NJ 07653. *Sewing machines and sergers.*

Singer Sewing Co., 200 Metroplex Dr., Edison, NJ 08818. *Sewing machines, presses, overlock machines.*

VWS, Inc., 11760 Berea Road, Cleveland, OH 44111-1601. (216) 252-2047. *Both Viking and White sewing machines, sergers, and presses.*

CUTTING TABLES

Bernina of America, Inc. *See Sewing Machines, above.*

Daynell, 1017 S. W. Morrison, Portland, OR 97205. (800) 222-5106. *Folding cardboard table.*

Sew/Fit Company, P.O. Box 565 La Grange, IL 60525. *Folding cardboard table.*

PATTERNS

Burda Patterns, P.O. Box 2517, Smyrna, GA 30081. *European patterns.*

Fashion Blueprints, 2191 Blossom Valley Dr., San Jose, CA 95124. *Ethnic patterns.*

Folkwear Patterns, P.O. Box 355, Newtown, CT 06470-9989. *Recently bought by Threads Magazine. Ethnic patterns.*

Great Fit Patterns, 221 SE 197th Ave., Portland, OR 97233. *Women's patterns size 38-60.*

Kwik Sew Pattern Co., 3000 Washington Ave. North, Minneapolis, MN 55411. *Patterns.*

Marge Murphy Heirloom Quilting Designs, P.O. Box 6306, Biloxi, MS 39532. *Patterns, silk batting.*

Stretch and Sew Patterns, P.O. Box 185, Eugene, OR 97440. *Patterns, knits, and interfacings.*

That Patchwork Place, Inc., P.O. Box 118, Bothell, WA 98041. *Quilting books and patterns.*

Toby O Creations, 59 Hamlet Rd., Levittown, NY 11756. *Collar pattern, Catalog $1 + SASE.*

INTERFACING

Dritz Corp., P.O. Box 5028, Spartanburg, SC 29304. *Interfacings and other sewing notions.*

Handler Textile Corp., 450 Seventh Ave., New York, NY 10123. (212) 695-0990. *Dress forms 6-46. Interfacing.*

HTC-Hendler Textile Corp., Consumer Products Division, 450 7th Ave., New York, NY 10123. *Interfacings.*

J & R Interfacings, c/o Dritz Corp., P.O. Box 5028, Spartanburg, SC 29304. *Interfacings and specialty fabrics.*

Sources of Supplies

Pellon Company Limited Partnership, Consumer Products Dept., 119 W. 40th St., New York, NY 10018. (212) 391-6300. *Interfacings.*

Staple Sewing Aids, 141 Lanza Ave., Garfield, NJ 07026. (800) 631-3820. *Interfacings.*

Therm Web, Inc., 112 W. Carpenter Ave., Wheeling, IL 60090. *Heat'n'Bond, fusible tapes for ribbon.*

NOTIONS AND SUPPLIES

Aardvark Adventures, Box 2449, Livermore, CA 94550. *Glitz threads, beads, shishas, creative books. Catalog $1.00.*

B&J Fabrics, 263 W. 40th St., New York, NY 10018. *Unusual novelty fabrics. Mail order, $15 minimum.*

Baer Fabrics, 515 E. Market St., Louisville, KY 40202. (800) 788-2237 ext. 170.

Bazaar Del Mundo, 2754 Calhoun St., San Diego, CA 92110. *Shisha mirrors, unusual trims and fabrics.*

Britex Fabrics, 146 Geary St., San Francisco, CA 94108. *$5 swatches.*

Cabin Fever Calicos, P.O. Box 550106, Atlanta, GA 30355. *Quilt books, notions, fabrics, batting.*

Celtic Design Company, 834 West Remington Drive, Sunnyvale, CA 94087. *Bias bars.*

Clotilde, Inc., 1909 SW First Ave., Ft. Lauderdale, FL 33315. *Threads, books, videos, needles, pins, notions, Ultrasuede scraps, generic sewing machine feet. Free catalog.*

Coats & Clark, 30 Patewood Plaza, Suite 351, Greenville, SC 29615. Attention: Meta Hoge. *Write for retail sales locations or consumer information.*

The Cotton Patch, 1025 Brown Ave., Lafayette, CA 94549. (415) 284-1177. *Quilting supplies and books.*

Dorr Mill Store, P.O. Box 88, Guild, NH 03754-0088. *100% wool in solid colors. $3 for two color charts.*

Dover Street Booksellers, P.O. Box 1563, 39 E. Dover St., Easton, MD 21601. *Extensive selection of books.*

Exotic Silks, 252 State St., Los Altos, CA 94022. *Wholesale silks.*

The Fabric Carr, P.O. Box 32120, San Jose, CA 95152. (415) 948-7373. *Professional Ironing supplies, sewing notions, books.*

G Street Fabrics, 12240 Wilkins Ave., Rockville, MD 20852. (800) 333-9191. *All fabrics mail order, custom service. $2 swatch service.*

Gladstone Fabrics, 16 W. 56th St., New York, NY 10019. *Metallic brocades, sequined fabrics, and more. Supplies for theatrical costumes. Mail order with $10 minimum.*

Gordon Button Co., Inc., 142 W. 38th St., New York, NY 10018. *Buttons, ornaments, and buckles.*

Greenberg & Hammer, Inc., 24 W. 57th St., New York, NY 10019. (212) 246-2835. *Notions, patterns, silk threads, scissors, professional irons and more. Mail-order catalog, $15 minimum.*

Hancock Fabrics, 3841 Hinkleville Rd., Interstate 24, Peducah, KY 42001. (800) 626-2723 ext. 456. *Gingher, Hobbs.*

The Hands Work, P.O. Box 386, Pecos, NM 87552. *Handmade and washable buttons. $2 catalog.*

Hersh 6th Avenue Buttons, Inc., 1000 6th Ave., New York, NY 10018. (212) 391-6615. *Large selection of dressmaking, millinery notions, and tools.*

Iowa Pigskin Expressions, 9185-210 St., Walcott, IA 52773. (319) 391-0107.

Jehlor Fantasy Fabrics, 730 Andover Park West, Seattle, WA 98188. (206) 575-8250. *Lamé, trims, beads, and sequins. $3.50 for catalog ($2.50 refundable with first order).*

Keepsake Quilting, P.O. Box 1459, Meredith, NH 03253. (603) 279-3351. *Books, notions, fabrics, lamé samples, batting.*

Kieffer's Lingerie Supplies, 1625 Hennepin Ave., Minneapolis, MN 55403. *Notions, lingerie fabrics, lace, notions.*

Lacis, 2990 Adeline, Berkeley, CA 94703. *New and antique laces. $1.50 for catalog.*

M&J Trimming Company, 1008 6th Ave., New York, NY 10018. (212) 391-9072. *Huge selection of trims and embellishments. Mail order with $50 minimum.*

Madeira USA Ltd., 30 Bayside Ct., Laconia, NH 03247-6068. *High quality threads, yarns, and flosses.*

Nancy's Notions, Ltd., P.O. Box 683, Beaver Dam, WI 53916. *Books, videos, notions, fabrics, fusibles. Free catalog.*

Newark Dressmaker Supply, Box 2448, Lehigh Valley, PA 18001. (215) 837-7500. *Mail-order source for almost all sewing supplies. Free catalog.*

Lew Novik, Inc., 45 W. 38th St., New York, NY 10018. *Large selection of metallic novelty fabrics, laces, ribbons, and more.*

C. M. Offray & Sons, Inc., Rt. 24, Box 601, Chester, NJ 07930-0601. *Ribbon.*

Poli Fabrics, 132 W. 57th St., New York, NY 10019. (212) 245-7589. *Almost all natural-fiber fabrics.*

Yvonne Porcella Studios, 3619 Shoemake Ave., Modesto, CA 95351. *Pieced clothing, printed clothing, variations, jacket patterns. SASE for information.*

Quilters' Resource, Inc., P.O. Box 148850, Chicago, IL. 60614. *Lamés, all types of threads and glitz supplies.*

QuiltSmith, Ltd., 252 Cedar Road, Poquoson, VA 23662. *ARDCO metal templates and rulers. SASE for catalog.*

Rosebar, 455 Oehler Pl., Carlstadt, NJ 07072. (201) 438-8825.

Rosen and Chadick, 246 W. 40th St., New York, NY 10018. *Imported and designer fabrics, bridal, lace, velvets, lamé, and more.*

Sources of Supplies

Margaret Schwanck, 7642 Washington Ave. South, Eden Prairie, MN 55344. *Ribbon floss.*

Seattle Fabrics, 3876 Bridge Way N., Seattle, WA. 98103. (206) 632-6022. *Outdoor fabrics. $3 price list.*

Sew Art International, P.O. Box 550, Bountiful, UT 84010. *Invisible thread, other unusual threads.*

Sew-Fit Co., P.O. Box 565, La Grange, IL 60525. (708) 579-3222. *Notions and accessories. Modular tables for sewing and books. Free catalog.*

Sewing Emporium, 1087 Third Ave., Chula Vista, CA 92010. (619) 420-3490. *Notions and accessories. Catalog $2.*

Sheru Enterprises, Inc., 49 W. 38th St., New York, NY 10018. (212) 730-0766. *Supplies for crafts, beading, macramé, sew-on and glue-on jewels, sequins, and more. Mail order with a $35 minimum. Catalog.*

So-Good, Inc., 28 W. 38th St., New York, NY 10018. (212) 398-0236. *This store sells all sorts of ribbons and trims. Mail-order catalog, $25 minimum.*

Speed Stitch, 3113-D Broadpoint Drive, Harbor Heights, FL 33983. *Sulky metallic threads, invisible threads, Sulky rayon threads, machine embroidery supplies. Catalog $3 (refundable with purchase).*

Steinlauf and Stoller, Inc., 239 W. 39th St., New York, NY 10018. (800) 637-1637. *Large selection of threads, snaps, trims, tools, interfacings, and more. $30 minimum or $5 service charge.*

Marinda Stewart, P.O. Box 402, Walnut Creek, CA 94596. *Specialty garment patterns, punch-needle books.*

Swiss-Metrosene, Inc., 1107 Marlin Dr., Roseville, CA 95661. *Threads.*

June Tailor, Inc., P.O. Box 208, Richfield, WI 53076. *Pressing and ironing equipment.*

Tandy Leather, P.O. Box 2934, Dept. 1191, Ft. Worth, TX 76113. *$1 catalog.*

Thai Silks, 252 State St., Los Altos, CA 94022. (800) 722-SILK.

Things Japanese, 9805 NE 116th St., Kirkland, WA 98034. *Tire silk twist and other specialty threads.*

L.P. Thur Designer Fabrics, 126 W. 23rd St., New York, NY 10011. *Large selection of spandex and budget fabrics. Mail order with $20 minimum.*

Tinsel Trading Co., 47 W. 38th St., New York, NY 10018. (212) 730-1030. *A wonderful store to find antique gold and silver trims. Also sells real gold and silver threads. Mail order with $25 minimum.*

Treadleart, 25834 Narbonne Ave., Lomita, CA 90717. (213) 534-5122. *Decorative and utility machine threads. $3 catalog. $18/year magazine, $3 sample issue.*

Trebor Textiles, 251A W. 39th St., New York, NY 10018. *Designer fabrics at discount prices.*

Ultra Scraps, P.O. Box 98, Farmington UT 84025. (801) 451-6361. *$1 catalog.*

Utex Trading, 710 9th St., Ste. 5, Niagara Falls, NY 14301. (416) 596-7565 ext. 38. *Silks.*

Vermont Patchworks, P.O. Box 229, Shrewsbury, VT 05738. (800) 451-4044, (802) 492-3590. *Quilting supplies and books. $2 catalog.*

Wool Merchant, 2331 E. Crown Point Executive Dr., Charlotte, NC 28222. (800) 849-WOOL.

William Wawak Co., Box 59281, Schaumberg, IL 60159-0281. *Tailors' supplies, interfacings, linings, thread, leather, and more.*

Index